THE 7 PILLARS OF HABIT BUILDING

DISCOVER THE SECRET TO BREAKING BAD HABITS
AND BUILDING LASTING POSITIVE ONES
WITHOUT STRESSING OVER PERFECTION

THINKNETIC

CONTENTS

Your 60 Second Review Can Change Everything For Us

Whether you've just picked up this book or have already started reading, we'd love it if you could take just 1 minute to leave a quick review. It's as easy as scanning the QR code or following the short link below.

Your feedback—whether it's about the book's topic or your excitement to dive in—is incredibly important for us. Reviews not only offer us valuable feedback, but they also play a big role in shaping how this book reaches a broader audience.

If you'd like to go the extra mile, consider attaching a photo of the book—whether it's the cover or a glimpse of the content—making your review stand out to other readers.

Your review, even with just a few words and a quick photo, makes a world of difference. Thank you for being a part of this journey!

Christoph M. *Michael M.*

Founders of Thinknetic

Scan Me

Go to: t.ly/t7pohbr

Get 100% Discount
On All New Books!

Get ALL our upcoming eBooks for FREE
(Yes, you've read that right)
Total Value: $199.80*

You'll get exclusive access to our books before they hit the online shelves and enjoy them for free.

Additionally, you'll receive the following bonuses:

Bonus Nr. 1

Our Bestseller
Critical Thinking For Complex Issues
Total Value: $9.99

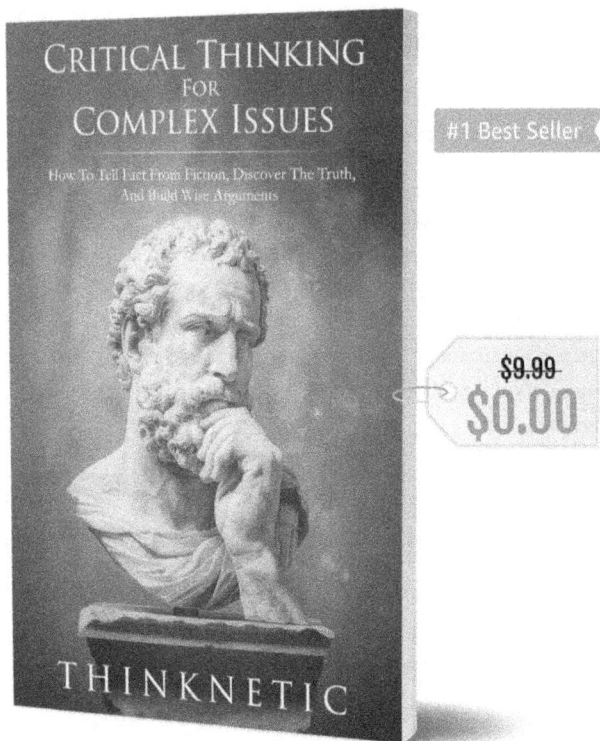

Are you tired of being manipulated by fake news and false arguments?

Arm yourself with the ultimate weapon - critical thinking.

Critical Thinking For Complex Issues is your guide to cutting through the noise and discovering the truth.

Learn how to spot logical fallacies, overcome confirmation bias, and analyze arguments objectively.

★★★★★

"Before this book, I kept falling for online rumors. Ugh! This book explains critical thinking in a way that's super easy to follow. Now I can easily tell what's real and what's fake. Bonus: I learned how to have good conversations, not just pointless arguments. This book is awesome!"

Yvonne - Reviewed in the United States on June 13, 2024

"This short (~300 pages) guide offers a timely challenge to become better thinkers by identifying mental pitfalls that even the best of us can fall into, and how to avoid them. Beginning with an overview of the value of critical thinking in our modern world, the guide then introduces the Socratic approach to asking questions, followed by a discussion on Rhetoric (creating a persuasive argument)."

Thomas Jerome Newton - Reviewed in the United States on July 2, 2024

"This book really helped me to not put trust in everything we might read or hear. Actually it helped me to see how valuable it is to question everything I read and hear. Look at the source, agenda of the information, biased or unbiased etc. Excellent read!"

Jared Szalkiewicz - Reviewed in the United States on June 25, 2024

"This book is very well written which makes it an easy read for those who choose to stray away from the normal path of what I would call herd thinking. Very insightful and provocative. I have already recommended this as a must read to my network of friends and family."

Paul Shelton Sr. - Reviewed in the United States on June 20, 2024

Bonus Nr. 2

Our Bestseller
The Intelligent Reader's Guide To Reading
Total Value: $9.99

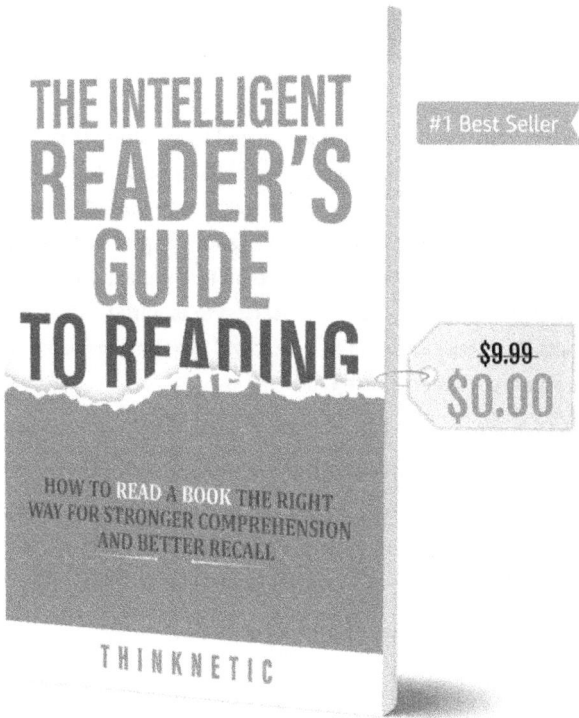

Ever feel like you've read a book but can't remember a single thing about it?

You spend hours pouring over pages, only to walk away with a vague sense of what you've consumed.

Imagine reading and actually remembering key arguments. Imagine truly understanding the author's message and discussing it with confidence.

This guide is your secret weapon.

★ ★ ★ ★ ★

"This is by far the best set of tools and strategies that I've read on improving reading. This is what I wished had been taught in Junior High. I've learned them by trial and error and see how they all fit together."

Michael McFarren - Reviewed in the United States on January 26, 2023

"It's been many years since I've started to regularly read books that I believe would help me grow. A challenge in doing so has been not having a systematic/strategic framework that will help me gain the most out of a book I've read. I'm glad to have found and read this, and after applying some techniques that I have learnt from this book, I already started to experience better results from my reading. I'm sure it will help you the same if you have similar challenge like I did.
Thanks to Thinknetic and its team for their good work!"

Sai Aung Lynn - Reviewed in the United States on April 23, 2023

"This book is very much practical. Straight to the point and concise. Comes with a lot of useful examples to build skills."

Amazon Customer - Reviewed in the United States on December 1, 2023

"I have read books of all types of genres for years. This book has clear and procise ways of reading to help one gain the most benefit out of their reading experience. I recommend all give it a good look there is something to learn for all."

Raymond E. Smith - Reviewed in the United States on March 2, 2023

Bonus Nr. 3 & 4

Thinking Sheets
Break Your Thinking Patterns
&
Flex Your Wisdom Muscle
Total Value Each: $4.99

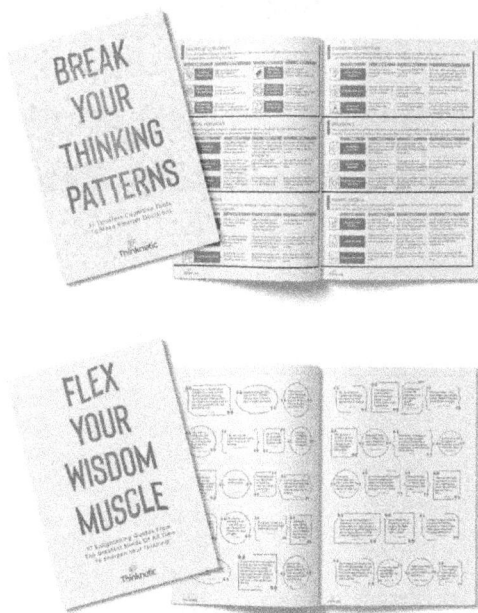

A glimpse into what you'll discover inside:
- How to expose the sneaky flaws in your thinking and what it takes to fix them (the included solutions are dead-simple)
- Dozens of foolproof strategies to make sound and regret-free decisions leading you to a life of certainty and fulfillment
- How to elevate your rationality to extraordinary levels (this will put you on a level with Bill Gates, Elon Musk and Warren Buffett)
- Hidden gems of wisdom to guide your thoughts and actions (gathered from the smartest minds of all time)

Here's everything you get:

✓ Critical Thinking For Complex Issues eBook   **($9.99 Value)**
✓ The Intelligent Reader's Guide To Reading eBook **($9.99 Value)**
✓ Break Your Thinking Patterns Sheet   **($4.99 Value)**
✓ Flex Your Wisdom Muscle Sheet   **($4.99 Value)**
✓ All our upcoming eBooks   **($199.80* Value)**

Total Value: $229.76

Go to the end of the book for the offer!

*If you download 20 of our books for free, this would equal a value of 199.80$

WHAT READERS ARE SAYING ABOUT THINKNETIC

"I wanted to read some books about thinking and learning which have some depth. I can say "Thinknetic" is one of the most valuable and genuine brands I have ever seen. Their books are top-notch at kindle. I have read their books on learning, thinking, etc. & they are excellent.

—Sahil Zen, 20 years old from India, BSc student of Physics

"Thinknetic provides excellent thought provoking and incisive books. They have a high rate of turnout and I am glad they have started doing audio books. I recommend their books to anyone wanting to improve themselves young or old. You are never too old to learn."

—Mike, 58 years old from Buckinghamshire (England), IT Consultant

"Thinknetic embodies an innovative and progressive educational approach, expertly merging deep academic insights with contemporary learning techniques. Their books are not only insightful and captivating but also stand out for their emphasis on practical application, making them a valuable resource for both academic learning and real-world personal development."

—Bryan Kornele, 55 years old, Software Engineer from the United States

"Thinknetic is a provider of books regarding mental models, thought processes, organizational systems, and other forms of mental optimization. The paradigmatic customer likely is to be someone in an early- to mid-career stage, looking to move up the ranks. Ultimately, though, the books could be of use to everyone from high school students to accomplished executives looking for ways to optimize and save time."

—Matthew Staples, 45, Texas (USA), Juris Doctor, Attorney

"I have been reading books from Thinknetic for a while now and have been impressed with the **CONDENSED AND VALUABLE INFORMATION** they contain. Reading these books allows me to **LEARN INFORMATION QUICKLY AND EASILY,** so I can put the knowledge to practice right away to improve myself and my life. I recommend it for busy people who don't have a **LOT** of time to read, but want to learn: Thinknetic gives you the opportunity to easily and quickly learn a lot of useful, practical information, which helps you have a better, more productive, successful, and happier life. It takes the information and wisdom of many books and distills and organizes the most useful and helpful information down into a smaller book, so you spend more time applying helpful information, rather than reading volumes of repetition and un-needed filler text.

—Dawn Campo, Degree in Human psychology and Business, Office administrator from Utah

"Thinknetic's works provide a synthesis of different books giving a very good summary and resource of self-help topics. I have recommended them to someone who wanted to learn about a topic and in the least amount of time."

—Travvis Mahrer, BA in Philosphy, English Teacher in a foreign country

"I have most of the ebooks & audiobooks that Thinknetic has created. I prefer audiobooks as found on Audible. The people comprising Thinknetic do an excellent job of providing quality personal development materials. They offer value for everyone interested in self-improvement."

—Neal Cheney, double major in Computer-Science & Mathematics, retired 25yrs USN (Nuclear Submarines) and retired Computer Programmer

"Thinknetic is a publishing house selling high-order practical books which are easily read and focus on key issues were basic principles are well-explained. They are great for Managers and business leaders - or those who aspire to these occupations or positions."

—Philip Atkinson, MSc in Organization Development,
Business consultant from the UK

INTRODUCTION

Do you feel like some people just seem to be better at keeping good habits than others? That while you struggle with the same loop of start, stop, and start again, they are continually making strides at every new thing they try? Are you tired of enthusiastically trying to make a new habit stick only to go back to your old ways a few days, weeks, or months later?

Habit building may come easier to some than others, but everyone still has to put in the effort to make habits work, at least at the beginning. What if, rather than habits simply coming naturally to certain people, those people were just doing things differently? More effectively?

Building good habits takes work. Cultivating a habit doesn't begin the second you start the behavior. No, habits start with the acknowledgment that something in your life needs changing. Whether it's an old habit from childhood that no longer makes sense, a coping mechanism that ultimately does more harm than good, or bad habits borne out of the path of least resistance, you must first identify the habit you want to break before you can change it and replace it with something better.

That's where this book comes in.

As you work through the chapters, you will learn the process of controlling your behaviors by changing things like your cues, your environment, and your support system. You will create a plan for success before you even begin, and then track your results so that you can analyze and assess them later. These are the seven pillars of habit building; the secrets to finally sustaining habits—making them stick!

We will also learn what to do if you try to incorporate a new habit into your life and fail, sliding right back into old, unwanted habits. Failure is something everyone deals with, and it's particularly common when we are learning something new. Dwelling on that failure is where the problems arise, so we have an entire chapter dedicated to getting you back on your feet after some missed attempts.

It wasn't until I started taking habit-building seriously that I began to see real progress in my life. While studying for my undergraduate degree, I realized that studying full-time while working evenings and weekends and fulfilling a teaching practicum required a strict schedule and positive habits to be successful. Those habits served me well years later when I returned to complete a Master's degree while pregnant and with a toddler at home!

As a teacher, writer, editor, and mother, my days can easily get away from me if I'm not intentional about how I want them to go. Finding time for healthy eating, exercise, mindfulness, family responsibilities, friends, work, professional development, and general self-care relies on a strict routine and lots of healthy habits. I am no stranger to the seemingly unending loop of breaking an old habit, starting a new one, and then sliding back into my old ways.

Although habits almost become automatic once they have been fully integrated into a daily routine, getting them to that point relies on several factors, including a detailed plan, tracking, and analyzing what's working and what isn't. It's important to me that I have a strong image of the person I want to be: healthy, strong, active, and present for my family, friends, and work so that I can make the right choices even when it would be easier not to. For me, that means taking a nightly walk, even when I would rather be streaming my favorite show or a 10-minute yoga video first thing in the morning, to get my day started on the right foot.

It doesn't mean I've got everything under control. I struggle with stress, interruptions due to illness, schedule changes, or just life getting in the way. I still battle with my own negative coping mechanisms, including procrastination! In the past decade, I have moved to three different countries, in three time zones, on two continents, and have had to adapt my habits to each new location. I have experienced my share of backsliding in certain areas from time to time as a result!

However, my ability to be flexible and adapt my habits to changing circumstances has improved dramatically since I began putting into place the principles found in this book consistently in my life.

One of those principles was finding my *personal support system*. It's easy to think that we're doing it all alone, but the truth is, there is a community out there for everyone, and it can make the difference between success and failure. Sometimes, that support system is in person, but other times, it's online.

Another principle involved incorporating *rewards* into my habit journey, something I neglected to do in the past. Doing so helped me to keep consistent with those habits that take time to see results, helping me choose them instead of the ones that offer instant gratification but nothing else of value. I have also learned to find the lesson in failure and apply it to my next attempt to implement the habit into my life.

If you have been frustrated in the past at your inability to cultivate habits that would bring long-term benefits in your life, this book is a great place to start over. Getting intentional about what you want in life increases your chances of making it happen.

You will learn about the habit loop, including cue, craving, behavior, and reward. We will discuss how to identify negative triggers and replace them with positive ones instead. You will understand how to adapt your environment to support your good habits, and how to find the support system and resources that will increase your chance of success. Finally, we will talk about how to cope if you slide back into old, unwanted habits.

Each chapter has exercises to get the momentum going, and the final chapter is a workbook that helps tie everything together. Think of using these pillars to architect your aspirations in life, one where you don't stress over perfection. I've designed this book to be both encouraging and no-nonsense, so that you have the tools you need to overcome every excuse, lack of motivation, and difficult circumstance in your path, as well as the tools to get back on track when you stumble.

If you're ready to put the habits in place that will significantly improve your quality of life, I'm excited that you've found this book. It's time to take control of your habits and start shaping the future you want for yourself. I can't wait for you to get started.

Kathleen Sperduti

1

THE BEAUTY OF BAD HABITS
HOW CAN SOMETHING SO BAD FEEL SO GOOD?

Rahul is jolted awake by the sound of his alarm at 6:30 a.m., as he is every weekday morning. His alarm first went off at 6:00 a.m., but Rahul has been snoozing it in ten-minute increments ever since, as he does every day. Unfortunately for him, 6:30 a.m. is the latest he can push off getting up if he wants to make it to work on time. He has been late so often that he is currently on probation with his manager. Any more late arrivals, he risks losing his job.

It may sound like Rahul oversleeps, but the truth is that he only averages about four hours of sleep on a good night. His problem isn't about getting up in the morning. His problem lies in his nighttime habits: Rahul is part of an online gaming community and regularly stays up until 2:00 a.m. or even 3:00 a.m. playing games online with his friends. He knows he should go to bed earlier to get more sleep, but he just can't seem to log off when he's having so much fun.

Rahul moved to a new city for work two years ago, leaving behind his circle of friends from college. Between his full-time job and volunteer work at an animal shelter, Rahul hasn't had much time for in-person socializing. Instead, he kept up the nightly habit of playing video games with them.

As soon as he connects with his buddies, he feels the day's stress falling away. The familiarity of the conversation holds none of the awkwardness he often feels when trying to get to know new people. He enjoys the easy banter, the excitement of the game, and the chance to forget that he lives far from home with few friends and a non-existent social life.

The problem is that his new city is in a time zone three hours ahead of his hometown. When he logs off at 3:00 a.m., it's only midnight for his friends back home. He knows that he should limit his gaming, but the fear of missing out and his loneliness contribute to his decision to log on nightly. He convinces himself that he will log off by midnight but gets so caught up in the game he never does. It feels so good to connect with his friends and to fall back into the same easy rhythm they had in college that he convinces himself he will have no trouble getting up the next morning.

Yet, every morning, the cycle continues. Rahul knows that he needs to change his nightly gaming habits, but nothing sticks. If he doesn't get this under control soon, he may lose his job. Not to mention, his health has been taking a toll. Rahul used to enjoy running 10k races but hasn't trained in months. He's too tired. He has been too tired to cook and instead relies on takeout for dinner. He has also been making silly mistakes at work, further straining his relationship with his boss.

Rahul understands that he needs to manage his nighttime gaming so he can get more sleep and function better during the day, but hanging out with his college friends online is the brightest spot of his day. It feels so good, yet it is causing problems in his day-to-day life. It isn't until Rahul learns about the habit loop that his behavior makes sense, and he is able to begin making the changes he needs to break free of his late-night gaming habit.

Have you ever engaged in a habit that you knew was bad for you, but you just couldn't seem to stop?

Why Do Bad Habits Make Us Feel Good?

As Rahul's story demonstrates, certain bad habits can be pleasing no matter how harmful you know them to be. It doesn't need to be as extreme as playing video games nightly into the wee hours of the morning, either. For example, starting each day with a cup of coffee on an empty stomach instead of eating breakfast is a typical bad habit that many people have. It can initially feel good to get those first sips of coffee, but later, you experience a burnout or crash midmorning when the caffeine is no longer keeping your energy up, and you haven't put any real fuel in your body in the form of a nutrient-dense breakfast.

It seems counterintuitive to think that our bad habits often win out when, logically, good habits, like enjoying a healthy breakfast, are better for us now and over time. Yet, that's often the case.

Why?

It is partly because a bad habit is often easier to start and sustain in the short term than a good habit. A quick jolt of caffeine in the morning provides an *immediate payoff* that preparing a nutritious breakfast might not. The good feeling Rahul gets from hanging with his friends online doing something he enjoys gives him an immediate positive consequence, rather than the delayed feeling of waking up rested the next morning. It is often the difference between instant and delayed gratification.

Bad habits can be particularly addictive because they often function as coping mechanisms. Some coping mechanisms are positive, but many are negative, including bad habits. Drinking excessive amounts of alcohol, illicit drug use, binge eating, or engaging in risky behavior are all examples of *negative coping strategies*. They feel good in the moment but are harmful over time. The vicious cycle of unhealthy coping reinforces bad habits. Repeating unhealthy behaviors eventually becomes a habit.

A *coping mechanism* is a psychological strategy used to manage stress, trauma, or difficult emotions.[1] They are sometimes employed when we lack functional problem-solving skills. *Positive coping mechanisms* foster long-term health and well-being, while *negative coping mechanisms* may feel good at the moment but ultimately cause more harm than good over time.

What Do Habits Have To Offer?

Habits can become almost unconscious once they have been ingrained into our routine. Research shows that over 40% of our daily activities are habits, done almost unconsciously, which frees up our brains for more onerous tasks.[2] As a result, they are "cognitively efficient," freeing up space in our brains to think about other things while still performing the habit regularly. Essentially, habits persist even after the motivation to perform it falls away, or the conscious thought to perform the habit disappears.

Is Your Childhood To Blame?

Many bad (and good!) habits are formed in childhood. At least one study shows that most children's habits and routines are set by age nine.[3] That doesn't mean that no habits are developed after that, but that the basic pattern for habit development typically stays the same as the child ages into adulthood.

Let's take a closer look at what this means: Young children's habits are typically first shaped by their primary caregivers. How the child's day was organized, whether there were set routines around mealtimes or bedtimes, and how children were taught emotional regulation in highly emotional situations—angry, sad, or struggling with a negative emotion or experience—are all forces that shape habits in childhood and into adulthood.

Think about your childhood. Were there set mealtimes in your home or rules around the foods that were available? Did your parents or caregivers comfort you with food or toys rather than teaching you to work through your emotions? Did you witness your parents engaging in healthy habits, such as getting regular exercise?

For many adults, the patterns they learned as children are the ones they carry with them into adulthood. You may not have developed a taste for caffeine as a child, but if you regularly went to school without breakfast, that could transform into the habit of only drinking a cup of coffee in the morning as an adult. If your parents comforted you with a bowl of ice cream or a piece of cake whenever you were upset, your tendency to "eat your emotions" as an adult is a logical extension of that habit.

Does that mean you are doomed to continue the cycle of negative habits you were exposed to as a child? No! It is possible to break out of the cycle of bad habits and replace them with good habits at any point in your life. It just takes a little work.

It is also important to note that not all bad habits are formed in childhood. Many people also tend to adopt unhealthy habits during stressful periods of life when they are unable to cope with stress in healthy ways. Often, what starts as a coping mechanism during a particularly tough period in our lives can turn into a long-lasting bad habit over time.

When Rahul first started playing online games with his friends late into the night, it was a way to cope with the loneliness of being in a new place and not knowing anyone. It developed into a bad habit of playing nightly and staying up so late that it affected his sleep, job, and health.

Habit Formation: The Short Version

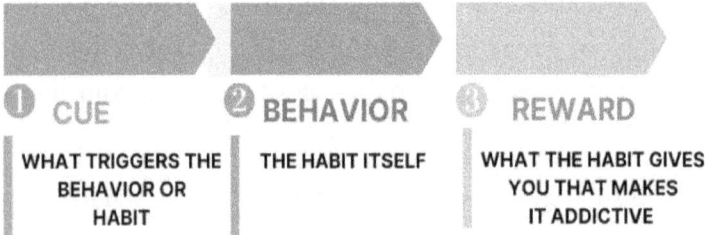

Habits, both good and bad, are formed in roughly the same way. We will dig deeper into this in later chapters, but the short version is that habits are formed by *Cue >Behavior >Reward.*[2]

Habit Formation

The Short Version

❶ CUE	❷ BEHAVIOR	❸ REWARD
WHAT TRIGGERS THE BEHAVIOR OR HABIT	THE HABIT ITSELF	WHAT THE HABIT GIVES YOU THAT MAKES IT ADDICTIVE

The *cue* is something that triggers the behavior or the habit. For example, for many people, getting out of bed in the morning is the *cue* for them to turn on the coffee pot. The *behavior* is the habit of drinking coffee first thing in the morning. Finally, the *reward* is what the habit gives you, making it addictive. The caffeine rush from the coffee makes you feel good almost immediately.[2]

So why are bad habits often so much easier to form and sustain than good ones? There are two main reasons:

1. *Bad habits are often easier to perform than good ones.* There are bad habits of omission, such as NOT doing something that would be good for you. Choosing not to floss your teeth or avoiding seeing the doctor regularly are bad habits requiring no effort on your part.

On the other hand, there are bad habits that are easier to do than good habits. Ordering a pizza for dinner three nights a week is easier than cooking a meal.

2. *Bad habits often offer immediate rewards.* The caffeine rush of a cup of coffee, the sugar rush of a cookie in the afternoon, or the relaxation of sitting on your couch rather than going to the gym all offer immediate or quick rewards. When our brain is rewarded immediately, it's easy to want to engage in the behavior repeatedly. All habits offer rewards, but immediate rewards can reinforce unwanted behaviors more easily than delayed ones. Breaking bad habits requires concentration and cognitive effort, which can be difficult when the incentives are not immediate or when the person is depressed, for example.[4]

Why Are Good Habits So Uncomfortable?

There are several reasons why adopting a new, good habit can be more difficult than adopting a bad or unhealthy habit.

1. *Lack of immediate reward*: We feel more rewarded by immediate pleasure than delayed pleasure. Many good habits have delayed rewards that take more willpower to push through in the early stages of habit formation, as the reward isn't immediately evident.[5] Starting the day with a short workout may have several health benefits, from increasing strength and flexibility to improving cardiovascular ability and potentially increasing longevity. Still, you may not see the benefits of that daily morning exercise routine for several months, making it more difficult to stick to it initially.

2. *Resistance to change*: We tend to repeat familiar and comfortable behaviors and avoid novel and challenging ones. If we already have an easy daily routine that provides immediate gratification, changing that routine for a delayed reward can seem overwhelming. We may need to create short-term rewards while we await the natural long-term rewards a new habit will eventually yield. This can also be time-consuming and mean more effort at the beginning when the change is already more difficult to make.

3. *Stress depletes self-regulation*: When stressed, the "path of least resistance" can be appealing. It is much easier to distract ourselves from our worries by binge-watching an entire season of our favorite show than spending an hour practicing yoga or meditating. Healthy activities usually require more self-control, which can feel more exhausting when we are already mentally tired or stressed.

4. *Personal challenges*: It takes more than just deciding to cultivate a healthy habit. It takes willpower, dedication, and a strategy to work through obstacles and setbacks. Sometimes, we struggle to find the mental strength it takes to work through those obstacles. Tiredness, insecurity, self-esteem, and health concerns are just some challenges to overcome when adopting more healthy habits. In the long run, building healthy habits will require addressing those issues. However, in the short term, behavioral and environmental changes are needed to create a solid foundation for change.

Conscious Change

Before we can change our habits, we need to be aware of them. That's the beauty of habit and the challenge when we want to change one. Once a habit is ingrained, it becomes automatic. Once it's automatic, we don't really have to think about it much. How often do you check your phone and scroll social media? Do you think about it first, or just do it?

To take stock of our habits and identify areas we want to change, we need to make the unconscious conscious. It gives us the upper hand, so to speak. As you move through this book, you will be guided to improve those habits you want changed. To do that, you must first be aware of your good and bad habits and identify the areas you want to tackle.

To help you get started, here's a list of some of the most common bad habits, along with a possible trigger and some reasons why they can feel so good at first. I also included a list of some of the most common good habits, including some reasons why they may feel so hard to adopt in the beginning. I hope these lists help you identify your habits.

Habit	Cue/Trigger	Reward/Why it feels good
Smoking	Coffee or work breaks	Nicotine causes the brain to release adrenaline
Binge-watching tv	After dinner or late-night routine	The brain releases dopamine
Eating excessive junk food or take-out	Friday night dinner	Comfort foods can be associated with happy memories
Impulse buying	Browsing certain websites	Can make us feel good about ourselves or minimize negative thoughts
Excessive drinking	Social outings or hanging with a certain group of friends	Can temporarily increase the body's dopamine and serotonin levels
Gossiping	Phone calls or texts from certain individuals	Triggers the chemical oxytocin, which promotes bonding with others
Spending too much time on social media	Boredom, idle hands	Can help people feel more connected and less isolated
Nail biting	Stressful situations, such as confrontation	Can provide something to focus on in times of stress
Oversleeping	The alarm goes off, hit snooze automatically	More rest when chronically sleep-deprived
Procrastination	Deadlines	Temporary relief from the stress or anxiety of the looming deadline

Table 1. Bad Habits

Habit	Cue/Trigger	Why it's hard
Morning workout	Morning alarm	Morning tiredness, still dark outside
Nutritious dinner	Arriving home from work	Not wanting to cook at the end of the day, fast food is easy to order
Getting 7-8 hours of sleep	Same bed and wake time daily	Distractions, social gatherings, wanting to stay up late
Limit screen time	Put the phone on do not disturb mode at the same time daily	Fear of missing out, a constant stream of new information
Walk 10,000 steps daily	Smartwatch reminder to move every hour	Can feel like an interruption or a nuisance at first
Meditate	Right after waking up or right before bed	Can be hard to settle the body and mind
Take a proper lunch break daily	Set an alarm or choose the same time to eat lunch daily	Work can get in the way; the work culture may be to eat at your desk while you work
Wear sunscreen daily	Apply after washing your face in the morning	Easy to forget or seem unnecessary, particularly in the winter months
Drink more water	Drink a glass of water every time you eat something	Water can be bland if you are used to drinking flavored drinks
Weekly check-in with a loved one	Schedule a weekly meetup or phone call	Finding a time when you are both available

Table 2. Bad Habits

Why should you care about the habits you form in your daily life? Whether you are reading this book because you are actively looking to change your personal habits, or because you are intrigued by self-improvement and want to know more, understanding your habits and taking control of the nature of the habits you cultivate in your life will be one of the best things you can do for the person you are and the one you want to become.

Action Steps

I will be including action steps at the end of each chapter so that you can put the information to work on your own. It is strongly encouraged that you take the time to work on the action steps at the end of each chapter before moving to the next, as they often build upon each other.

1. *Reflect on your childhood habits.* Make a list of the childhood routines and habits that you had before the age of ten. Consider mealtimes, bedtime routines, exercise habits, household chores, etc. Which bad habits from your childhood have continued into adulthood, directly or indirectly? Which good habits have you maintained?

2. *Make a list of your bad habits*, their cues, and why they make you feel good in the short term. Then, add a reason they may harm you over the long term.

3. *Make a list of your good habits,* their cues, and why they were difficult for you to start initially (if they were). Then, add how they are good for you in the long term.

4. *Make a list of five good habits you would like to cultivate.* Perhaps they involve breaking your current bad habits (e.g., if you are sedentary, you may want to incorporate 20 minutes of exercise daily), or perhaps they are entirely new habits.

Now that we understand why bad habits make us feel so good in the short term but are bad for us over time, we can identify those areas for improvement. In Chapter 2, we will learn to identify areas where bad habits have taken hold.

Chapter Summary

- Unhealthy, unhelpful, or bad habits may provide short-term gratification but ultimately cause long-term harm.
- Bad habits are not always about the actual habit but may be used as coping mechanisms for a trauma or a lack of functional problem-solving skills.
- Establishing healthy habits requires going through a period of discomfort before long-term benefits begin to show.
- Resistance to change, delayed gratification, and a need for greater self-control can make it hard to start and sustain good habits.
- Sustaining good habits requires consistent coping with the discomfort until the positive behaviors become automatic and the discomfort eases.

- Note that healthy, useful habits will feel uncomfortable for months, but the positive effects will add up and eventually become a source of motivation.

PILLAR 1 - SAY GOODBYE TO YOUR OLD SELF

START YOUR TRANSFORMATION TODAY THROUGH THE 3-HABIT FORMULA TO BUILD A BETTER YOU

S ophie was a chronic procrastinator. She had been that way since she was a child. If a class assignment was due Monday morning, Sophie could be found furiously typing away at her laptop late Sunday night. Her habit of procrastinating hadn't improved in adulthood; only the stakes were higher, and she found it harder to meet deadlines the way she could before. It affected every area of her life, and not in a good way.

Last year, Sophie took a personal day to finally finish filing her taxes by the deadline, a task she had put off until the very last minute. Instead of working on her taxes first thing in the morning, she spent an hour cleaning off her desk and filing some papers, put in a load of laundry, meal planned for the week, made a grocery list to go with it, and caught up on half a season of her favorite show. Finally, at 5:00 p.m., panicked that she wouldn't make the midnight filing deadline, Sophie finally sat down and started on her taxes.

That was the last straw. Sophie knew that her habit of procrastinating was holding her back and making her life more stressful than necessary, so she decided to do something about it. Sophie began by identifying the key areas that needed improvement, like setting priorities, finding motivation, and building self-discipline.

She conducted a personal SWOT analysis to identify her strengths, weaknesses, opportunities, and threats. Sophie used those findings to create SMART goals to help her overcome her bad habit of procrastinating. She then worked hard to meet the milestones she set for herself. Breaking the habit of procrastinating doesn't happen overnight.

Sophie began automating as many of the things that regularly caused her to procrastinate as she could. This meant automating bill payments and moving money to a savings account on a set date each month. Next, she identified the top three activities that caused her to procrastinate and made those her priority, tackling one activity a month. For Sophie, they included addressing her work inbox and returning emails, completing her monthly reports before the last minute, and getting in a daily workout. Once those areas were sorted, she moved on to the next three on her list.

A year later, Sophie is what she likes to call a 95% reformed procrastinator. She knows that the tendency to procrastinate will always be there, except now she has strategies in place to overcome the urge and get things done. She sets a timer when she can't resist a bit of procrastination, but once the alarm rings after five or ten minutes, she can focus on whatever needs to be done. As a result, Sophie's stress levels have dropped, her productivity has skyrocketed, and she has more free time to do the things she loves.

Every person is unique, and identifying key areas for improvement is essential for success. There's no "one-size-fits-all" when it comes to habits. The first pillar of habit building is understanding yourself and saying goodbye to the parcel of your identity holding you back. This chapter is designed to help you figure out your strengths and weaknesses and develop the self-awareness required to evaluate your behavior, productivity, and efficacy to discover what's holding you back so you can learn how to move forward.

The Importance Of Self-Awareness

Self-awareness falls into two broad categories: internal self-awareness and external self-awareness.

1. *Internal self-awareness*: This refers to how well we understand ourselves, including our thoughts, feelings, strengths, weaknesses, passions, and how we impact others.

2. *External self-awareness*: This refers to how well we understand how we are seen by others. [1]

While both types of self-awareness are important to cultivate, we will focus more on internal self-awareness and how making the effort to truly understand ourselves can lead to better choices and life habits.

Before we can really begin to make lasting changes in our lives, we need to take stock of where we are and what we are working with on a personal level. Awareness of our habits, including our cues, is the key to changing them. This chapter will walk you through the steps of analyzing your strengths and weaknesses, setting SMART goals, and determining your priorities so that you can focus on the right things.

Creating A Personal SWOT Analysis

SWOT stands for Strengths, Weaknesses, Opportunities, and Threats. The tool was originally designed to help businesses optimize performance and minimize risk by evaluating internal strengths and weaknesses, opportunities, and threats. It paints a comprehensive picture of where a business stands, which is then used to create an action plan. It is one of the "oldest and most adopted strategy tools worldwide.[2] However, it can also be applied to personal growth plans, which is what we will do here.[3]

When creating a personal SWOT analysis, it's recommended to follow the process separately for different areas of your life, as the strengths, weaknesses, opportunities, and threats may look very different.

Internal Factors

Strengths: These are the things you are good at and feel good about. Strengths can be general traits applicable across many areas of life or more specific skill-related items. Perhaps you are a strong communicator, negotiator, and detail-oriented at work, while as a parent, you are patient, fun, and compassionate.

Weaknesses: It can be hard to list our weaknesses, but it's important to be honest to get the most out of the exercise. It's about where we need to put our efforts to achieve our goals. Are you a people-pleaser who can't say no? Do you procrastinate? Strengths and weaknesses are what you bring to the table and have complete control over.

External Factors

Opportunities: Opportunities are those chances that we must act on to reap the benefits. Don't be afraid to look outside your comfort zone and identify things that may be intimidating. The purpose of a SWOT analysis is to encourage growth.

Threats: Identifying threats means understanding which battles must be fought and where you are most at risk. Threats may hold you back in the future. However, your immediate environment and the people in it can also be threats. If you can identify threats accurately, you can work to either neutralize them or turn them into opportunities.[3]

Common Areas Of Growth And Development

Everyone is different. The habits you might want to cultivate or the goals you want to achieve are not going to be the same as someone else's, but there are certain general areas of improvement that many people share.

The Five Common Areas Of Personal Growth

1. *Physical*: This relates to your physical well-being, including diet, exercise, sleep, and general physical health. Many people seek to improve one or more of these factors by cultivating healthy habits such as eating a nutritious diet or getting enough quality sleep nightly.

2. *Mental*: This relates to mental health, stress, how you think and learn, your mindset, and mental toughness. Unhealthy habits and lifestyle choices can increase stress levels.[4] Learning to manage stress, improving executive functioning skills, or practicing mindfulness can improve your mental health. Developing healthy habits, such as learning a new skill or implementing stress-relieving practices, is a common goal.

3. *Emotional*: This focuses on how you identify and process your emotions, including how you react in stressful situations and control the urge to have emotional outbursts. Practicing healthy habits such as journaling, talking to a therapist or counselor, or taking a course on conflict-resolution skills can increase emotional health and well-being.

4. *Social*: Social skills are essential for building and maintaining strong personal and professional relationships. Many of these skills center around good communication, including active listening and communicating ideas clearly and respectfully.

5. *Spiritual*: Spiritual growth involves connecting with yourself on more than just the physical level. For some, organized religion fills that need, while for others, a connection to nature or the universe suffices. Some habits to consider include finding time to meditate or pray, spending time with nature, or studying sacred books.[5]

The Eisenhower Matrix

Did you read the section above and feel slightly overwhelmed at the idea of tackling five different areas of personal development at once? Don't worry! The reality is that trying to change multiple things in your life simultaneously is not the best plan. The key is to decide which items you should focus on first and then take it from there. This is where the Eisenhower Matrix can be helpful. The matrix was designed based on a study of President Eienhower's time management style, separating the merely urgent from the important. Studies have shown that many people have difficulty separating truly important tasks from those that are merely urgent.[6]

Stephen Covey popularized it in his book *The 7 Habits of Highly Effective People.*[7]

It is a simple and effective tool to prioritize tasks and manage time. The matrix is based on the principle that not all tasks are equally important or urgent and that you should focus on the ones that matter most by categorizing your tasks into one of four categories that are a mix of urgent, not urgent, important, and not important. By categorizing your tasks and priorities under these four categories, you can decide which to tackle immediately, which to schedule to do soon, which to delegate to someone else if possible, and which to delete. This is a tool to help with time and habit management.

The categories are:

1. *Urgent/Important*: These are the items you should prioritize, as they are important but also urgent, meaning they should be handled as quickly as possible. They can include projects with urgent deadlines at work, lifestyle changes based on a medical diagnosis, or even something unexpected like a flat tire. Any task that MUST be done now or has clear consequences in the short term falls under this category.

2. *Not Urgent/Important*: People often procrastinate on these tasks because, despite their importance, they don't feel urgent. These tasks have long-term benefits but not short-term satisfaction, a bit like the good habits we discussed in Chapter 1. Regular exercise, spending time with family, eating healthy, and career planning are all important but don't always feel urgent in our day-to-day lives. This quadrant is where you should focus your energy most days.

3. *Urgent/Not Important*: These items can often be pushed back or delegated in some way. If you have ever been interrupted at work by multiple phone calls or emails that feel urgent but don't require an immediate response, they fall into this category. Any type of interruption or distraction that doesn't qualify under the terms of category 1, urgent and important, belongs here. This category can be controlled in large part by setting boundaries or delegating where possible.

4. *Not Urgent/Not Important*: Whenever possible, items that fall into this category should be reduced or even eliminated. This includes activities that waste your time or are used to procrastinate. This doesn't mean you can never play a game on your phone or catch up with a colleague at work, but when these activities are cutting into the time needed for more important items, it's time to set some boundaries.[7]8

Urgent/Important	Not Urgent/Important
Urgent/Not Important	Not Urgent/Not Important

The Matrix

How does this work in real life? You should fill out the matrix daily to see if it needs adjusting. Let's say your long-term goal is to participate in a 5km run for a charity that is close to your heart six months from now. The problem? You can't even walk 5km, let alone run it! The goal of a 5km run in six months is important but probably doesn't feel urgent yet.

You can use the matrix to prioritize your training so that when the race is two weeks away, you aren't in a panic because you haven't yet started training. In the *important and urgent* box, you should prioritize buying a pair of running shoes and a comfortable running outfit if you haven't yet. Then, download a training program designed to get you to your goal within the time frame allotted.

In the *important but not urgent* box, you should choose your training schedule based on the program you choose to follow. Put the dates and times in your calendar and clear your schedule.

To do that, look at your *urgent but not important* box to see which items can be scheduled for a later date or delegated to someone else to free up more training time. Finally, be honest about the types of activities you use as distractions or time-wasters in your *not important and not urgent* box. Which can you easily minimize or eliminate?

Get SMART About Your Goals

SMART goals are one of the most popular methods for achieving big goals. Dreaming big is easy, but achieving those dreams through effective goal-setting and monitoring is hard work. That's where SMART goals shine. They help break down big goals into measurable chunks, making continued forward movement less overwhelming.

SMART stands for Specific, Measurable, Achievable, Relevant, and Time-Bound. SMART goals take vague ideas and clarify them to make them achievable. Perhaps you want to be "more productive" at work or are trying to "eat healthier." The SMART system will guide you in identifying tangible measures that you can objectively track and measure for success.[9]

Specific: Each SMART goal must be specific. "More productive" at work is too vague. What would greater productivity look like for you? Perhaps better productivity would mean being able to leave work by 6:00 p.m. at least three nights a week. Or perhaps you would like to bring work home no more than twice a month.

Likewise, "eat healthier" doesn't mean anything concrete. What would eating healthier look like for you? Maybe you want to start by eating breakfast at home daily rather than stopping at a drive-thru for coffee and donuts every morning. Or maybe it means eating fruit or vegetables at every meal.

Next, choose dates by which you would like to achieve those goals. It may not be possible to leave at 6:00 p.m. each night right from the start. A timeline keeps you on track and lets you see if you are moving closer to achieving your goals.

An important piece to remember when setting SMART goals is that a large goal may require multiple smaller milestones or multiple units of measurement to be successful. This can help you see exactly which areas are going well and which need more attention or tweaking to keep on track. For example, if your goal is to eat a fruit or a vegetable at each meal, you might break that goal down. Perhaps you can start by including a serving of fruit with breakfast each day for a month. Once that becomes a habit, add in a serving of fruit or vegetable at lunch, and so on.

Measurable: How are you going to manage your progress? Setting a goal without a mechanism for keeping track is counterproductive. Once the initial excitement of starting something new wears off, measuring milestones can keep you moving forward. Likewise, measurable milestones allow for flexibility in reassessing goals regularly rather than all or nothing. Success can be measured in a variety of ways. A simple checklist is perhaps the most common and is included in most habit trackers. How many mornings over the last 30 days did you eat a piece of fruit for breakfast?

Measurement tools can also include measures of productivity, such as keeping track of how many repetitions of a specific exercise you perform each workout session or how many pages of your novel you write weekly.

If your goal is to leave work by 6:00 p.m. nightly, but your boss is used to you pulling late nights at the office regularly, you may need to cut back incrementally. This is partly to ensure that you can still get all your work done on time and give your colleagues and boss time to adjust to your new shorter days.

Setting a goal of leaving by 6:00 p.m. nightly within five months means you must leave earlier, only one night a week during the first month. If you look back at the end of the month and realize you only left on time one week out of four, you know you aren't on track to meet your goal. Allowing for flexibility may mean recognizing that there are periods during the fiscal year when this won't be possible and scheduling those exceptions into your plan.

Achievable: Big dreams are wonderful, but you need to ensure that they are achievable. That doesn't mean shrinking your ambitions. It means setting achievable milestones that build upon each other until you reach your dream. If your "healthy eating" goal in your mind really means eating all whole foods, no sugar, additives, or dyes, with each meal prepared at home, chances are you will struggle to achieve that sustainably within one or two months.

You may be able to manage it for a short, challenging period, but maintaining it for life would involve a scaffolded approach that works by making incremental changes over time. Cutting out added sugar might be the first step.

Setting smaller, more achievable goals that can be used as a foundation for continued growth is preferable to setting one huge goal that quickly becomes overwhelming and is later abandoned.

Relevant: Make sure the milestones are relevant. Avoid getting stuck on details that distract from what is important. You don't need to completely rearrange your workspace and buy all new office supplies to be more productive, nor do you need a kitchen full of fancy gadgets to make breakfast at home each morning. Focus on what's important, and don't procrastinate on getting started. Circumstances need not be perfect to begin.

Time-bound: Part of keeping yourself accountable is having specific milestones and deadlines. In our examples, we have set five months to be able to leave nightly at 6:00 p.m. from work by meeting monthly milestones of leaving earlier one night per week for one month and adding in an additional night each subsequent month. In our eating healthy goal, it would take three months to achieve the goal of eating a fruit or vegetable at each meal. The plan starts with adding a fruit to breakfast each day for one month, before adding a fruit or vegetable at lunch the next, and finally adding one to dinner.

Again, flexibility is important. You may need to re-evaluate occasionally, but if you don't have milestones and a timeline to achieve your goals, you may not realize that you aren't near meeting your bigger goal until it's too late for course correction. If you are already wondering, "What happens if I am unable to follow these strategies?" don't worry! We will be tackling how to get back on track if we fall off the good habit wagon in Chapter 9.

Action Steps

1. *Conduct a Personal SWOT Analysis.*

Are there specific strengths or weaknesses you can associate with the good and bad habits you listed in Chapter 1?

2. *Based on your SWOT analysis, choose two to four areas of your life you would like to improve.*

Answer the following questions for each: Why this particular area? How would improving this area change my life for the better? What habits do I have that would help? What habits would I need to cultivate?

3. *Get SMART.*

Using the areas of your life you chose to improve in the action step above, set SMART goals for achieving them. Which actions and habits will help you reach them?

Now that we have identified our key areas to focus on, the hard work begins. Conquering negative habits is the first step to making the important changes that will benefit your life now and in the future. Chapter 3 is about removing the negative so we can put our energy where it belongs, on the positive.

Chapter Summary

- A personal SWOT analysis (Strengths, Weaknesses, Opportunities, and Threats) can provide a structured approach to personal improvement and growth.
- Effective goal setting is key to achieving your dreams. They increase the likelihood of following through and being successful.
- The Eisenhower Matrix helps you sort daily activities into four quadrants: Urgent/Important, Not Urgent/Important, Urgent/Not Important, and Not Urgent/Not Important.
- Use the Eisenhower Matrix to identify which areas of your life you should spend more time on

and delegate or eliminate unimportant time-wasters.

- SMART Goals are goals that are Specific, Measurable, Achievable, Relevant, and Time-bound.

PILLAR 2 - WHO'S CALLING THE SHOTS?

TARGET NEGATIVE TRIGGERS AND TAKE AIM IN CONTROLLING BAD HABITS TO CREATE IMMEDIATE POSITIVE CHANGE

A rmindo didn't consider himself a smoker. Not really. He didn't carry around a pack of cigarettes everywhere he went. Instead, he smoked socially. He started in college when his friends would hang out in bars and off-campus apartments. The social smoking habit stuck even after getting a full-time job when he would meet up with his college buddies twice a month.

Except recently, Armindo realized that he had started to smoke on his work breaks as well. He hadn't realized how often he asked his colleagues for a cigarette until one of them jokingly told him he would soon owe everyone a pack. In his mind, he had still been smoking occasionally —the way he used to in college.

When he sat down to do the math, Armindo realized he was smoking at least two cigarettes a day during his weekday breaks and at least another four or five over the weekend. Fourteen or fifteen cigarettes a week is a *habit*, not an occasional indulgence, and Armindo decided that it was time to stop smoking altogether.

The trouble is, smoking was associated with some of Armindo's best memories: late nights partying with friends, relaxed summer BBQs, study sessions in college, and even relaxing with his new work friends. The act of smoking was so entwined with his social identity that Armindo wasn't sure how to stop the behavior while still maintaining the relationships he had fostered over a pack of cigarettes. Still, he was determined to try.

Bringing Your Negative Triggers Into The Light

This chapter might be tough. In it, you will be asked to identify your personal negative triggers that can deflect or block the adoption of good habits and lead to bad habits or coping mechanisms instead. Some negative triggers might be associated with good memories but lead to bad habits, like Armindo's growing smoking habit. Other negative triggers may be mildly upsetting, such as an embarrassing memory or a somewhat hurtful experience. Still, others may be more serious and bring up more difficult or traumatic memories. Be gentle with yourself and only work on as many triggers as you can in a healthy way, one at a time.

You may need to come back to this chapter more than once. It's fine to tackle one trigger at a time if that's what you need to do. The goal is to keep moving forward, even if it means doing so slowly. One of the salient pillars of habit building is understanding triggers. As the second pillar, this chapter focuses on removing the influences that get in the way of healthy activities, establishing a self-check system, and accumulating positive associations and results that further encourage positive habits.

What Is A Negative Trigger, Anyway?

A *trigger* is an environmental factor, such as a person, place, thing, or time, that elicits an emotion. Negative triggers can often make us want to turn to coping mechanisms to manage how they make us feel. We may, over time, reach for the same coping mechanism repeatedly, creating a habit.

What happens in our body and mind in response to a trigger? A common concept in Cognitive Behavioral Theory explains the different reactions triggers provoke, often referred to under the acronym *BEST:* Behaviors, Emotions, Sensations, otherwise known as Physical Feelings, and Thoughts.[1,2] We react to a trigger in one or more of the above four ways.

Behavior: The actual behavior the trigger evokes. This is the visible habit. For many people, drinking a cup of coffee is a cue to smoke a cigarette. For others, brushing their teeth is a cue to floss as well. For school children, the school bell at the end of the day is their trigger for packing up their books and going home.

Emotions: Does a trigger make us feel happy, angry, anxious, nervous, or sad? When a trigger provokes certain emotions, we may be tempted to reach for a coping mechanism to manage it.

Sensations: These are the physical feelings that pop up in response to a trigger. Have you ever felt your body tense up or your face flush in response to a trigger? That falls under this category.

Thoughts: Negative triggers can often set off a variety of thoughts that we can have difficulty controlling. When the thoughts are negative, it can lead to self-doubt, self-loathing, or a desire to engage in an activity that gets rid of those thoughts, even temporarily.

Armindo associated smoking with the good feeling that comes with relaxing and connecting with friends. As a result, whenever he found himself in a social situation in which people were smoking, he physically craved a cigarette *(Sensations)*. He imagined the way smoking made him feel, and a feeling of relaxation came over him *(Thoughts, Emotions)*. He then asked someone for a smoke *(Behaviors)*.

The human brain creates unconscious patterns of thoughts and associations with previous experiences, so we unconsciously feel that repeating a behavior in a certain situation will produce the same result as the previous one. If the result is positive, the association becomes positive, but if the result is negative, we likely want to avoid repeating the behavior. The problem is that sometimes people associate those habits as positive, even when the outcome is actually harmful. Armindo feels as though smoking is a relaxing social habit, even if it poses serious health risks over time.

This pattern isn't always specific to negative behaviors. If a person has a traumatic association with a healthy behavior, they may follow the same pattern. While the habit may feel good in the short term, it is actually negative over the long term.

Identifying Negative Triggers

Identifying your negative triggers moves beyond simply identifying the cues you use to engage in unhealthy or bad habits. It means that you need to look beneath the surface to figure out what is going on. The next few chapters will be about working through these triggers to get to the good part of creating better habits.

Since habits become actions that we engage in often almost unconsciously, identifying your triggers and the reasons behind them means playing detective in your own life by not only observing your behaviors but identifying the BEST factors (behaviors, emotions, sensations, or thoughts) behind them. It is only when you get to the heart of the payoff or reward of the habit that you will be able to understand what is causing you to repeat even the least helpful behaviors.

This understanding will help you better control your behavior. How do you feel immediately after succumbing to an unhealthy trigger? Does that habit help, or does it make you feel worse? What habits do you engage in that block your success?

The good news about identifying your triggers is that the change in your thinking can be immediately noticeable. Once you become aware that bad habits don't produce the comforting results you're hoping for, you can work on breaking them. *Reducing unhelpful behavior* to a great degree is possible right away, as you can exert self-control over behaviors by becoming conscious of the triggers.

This can sound simple, but in practice, it can be very difficult. It takes three main steps.

1. *A moment of awareness*: Much of this chapter has been about this. The first step to change is recognizing the trigger and how it typically makes you think, feel, and behave.

2. *The ability to resist urges*: This is perhaps the toughest of the three steps. It's one thing to understand your triggers and how they impact your behavior intellectually. It's another to resist the urge to react the same way and make space for a better alternative. As we learned earlier, the immediate payoff is easier to succumb to than delayed gratification.

3. *A replacement behavior*: If you aren't going to do what you've always done, what then? Having one or more replacement behavior options prepared in advance, like

Armindo's chewing gum, can help resist those urges until the new behavior becomes a habit.[3]

Armindo has realized that he is smoking more than occasionally. He realizes that his smoking is tied to social situations. Smoking during work breaks is a new habit, so he starts there. Though he doesn't want to give up spending breaks with colleagues forever, for the first few weeks, he skips break time altogether to help break the habit.

The bad news is that completely breaking bad habits is one thing, but *cultivating new good habits* takes more time. It is often said that it takes 21 days to form a new habit, but that number is not based on any actual studies. A 2009 study showed that habit formation can take anywhere between 18 to 154 days. The average time to form a habit was 66 days.[4] Only, the number of days isn't the only factor. Some habits take longer to form than others. The less effort a habit takes, the quicker it typically forms. Incorporating a glass of water at each meal is easier to make a habit, say, than working out five days a week.

Self-awareness supports gradual, sustainable improvement in exercising willpower, refraining from unhealthy behaviors, and fostering new ones. It no longer feels overwhelming to put a plan in place to avoid or reconfigure your triggers for a more positive outcome.

That's why it's positive that Armindo took things in stages since he felt the need to. When he thought he was ready, he rejoined his colleagues during their breaks, armed with chewing gum or a small snack to take his mind off smoking. The first couple of days were hard, but Armindo soon enjoyed the company of his colleagues without reaching for a cigarette. He then felt ready to let his college buddies know that he was no longer a smoker during their next night out and would be ready with some strategies to help it stick.

When Triggers Are Actually Traumatic Or Self-Destructive

Sometimes, our habits are triggered by deeper issues or past experiences. Those habits can be survival mechanisms, or they can be dangerously self-destructive or even immediately hazardous to our health. If you are dealing with untreated trauma or feel that your habits require professional help to break, please seek out that help immediately. You don't have to do it alone, and there's no shame in asking for help when it's too much for you to handle.

Action Steps

1. *What are your top three negative triggers?* If you find it hard to identify your triggers at first, work backward. What are the three bad habits you would like to break the most?

2. *BEST.* Identify the BEST (Behavior, Emotions, Sensations, Thoughts) factors that those triggers set off in you.

- Trigger 1:

- Trigger 2:
- Trigger 3:

3. *What can you change immediately?* What is immediately possible to change for the better? Can you avoid or change the trigger? If not, can you change one of the BEST factors to avoid engaging in the negative habit? Any positive change is good.

Now that you have identified your negative triggers and worked to make the immediate changes to support a change in habits, Chapter 4 will help you switch from negative to positive triggers, giving you even more support in your quest to break bad habits and make new, better ones.

Chapter Summary

- Triggers are environmental factors that elicit an emotion, such as a person, place, thing, or time. Negative triggers can often make us want to turn to coping mechanisms to manage how they make us feel.
- BEST: Behaviors, Emotions, Sensations (otherwise known as Physical Feelings), and Thoughts (Outlook Associates). We react to a trigger in one or more of the above ways.
- Identifying triggers can result in an immediate positive change in thoughts and actions, but long-term habit changes take time to solidify.

- Breaking a bad habit requires awareness, resisting the urge to behave the same way as usual, and a replacement behavior instead.
- Know when a habit requires therapy or the help of a professional to break and seek out that help as soon as possible.

PILLAR 3 - THE ABCS OF HABIT MASTERY

SPELLBIND SUCCESS WITH THE ALPHABET OF BREAKING UNWANTED HABITS

Mary used to have a "junk" food addiction. She struggled for years with her tendency to overeat sugary, sweet, and even salty snacks in the evenings while relaxing after dinner. Her doctor was concerned about many of her health indicators, including her weight, cholesterol levels, and blood pressure. She was encouraged to improve her nutrition and be more active daily.

Determined to improve her health, Mary started each day ready to do better than the day before. Her days started with a nutritious breakfast, and she had high hopes that it was the start she needed to make the rest of the day follow suit. With her heels in her bag, she would put on her running shoes and head out to walk the fifteen minutes into work.

However, once she started her workday, things often went sideways. Mary's job was high-paced and stressful, and she would often skip lunch altogether or order something in, have a few bites, and let the rest go cold. The coffee pot in the break room became her go-to when she felt a dip in her energy levels, and she often consumed an entire pot of coffee on her own by the end of the day, each cup topped up with cream and sugar.

By 4:00 p.m., she was starving and craving something sweet. Heading out to the donut shop next door to the office became her afternoon ritual, and it wasn't unusual for her to eat two large donuts during her 20-minute break. The sugar rush felt good at first, but her energy crashed soon after, leaving her tired and cranky.

At home, too tired to cook, Mary frequently heated a frozen meal or ordered dinner. In the evenings, burnt out from the day, Mary spent the last few hours before bed streaming her favorite shows and mindlessly eating whatever was at hand—often chips, cookies, popcorn, ice cream, or brownies. Rather than stopping at a single serving, Mary regularly ate the entire package without realizing it until nothing was left.

Discouraged and frustrated with herself and her lack of self-control, Mary went to bed determined to do better the next day, only to repeat the same pattern over and over. Despite her best intentions, she just couldn't break her poor eating habits.

To break a habit we no longer want, we must first understand what triggers it. As we worked on in Chapter 3, we learned that bad or unwanted habits are usually an attempt to fulfill an unmet need that may not be obvious at first glance. Armindo's trigger for smoking was socializing with friends and colleagues. The habit gives our brain an immediate reward, even with negative long-term consequences.

The third pillar of habit building explores how we can instead create positive cues by associating good habits with meaningful rewards. Central to this is the alphabet of breaking unwanted routines. Armindo still wanted to socialize, but rather than reaching for a cigarette, he switched to chewing some gum or having a small snack. Triggers are the neurophysiological connections between cravings, feelings, and actions in connection to a situation or an experience. Fortunately, we can manipulate them to our advantage.

The ABC(DE) Model

The ABC Model is often used in cognitive behavioral therapy to help change the way someone responds to an event. It is also useful in breaking unwanted habits. This model helps us become aware of how our emotional experiences and thought patterns contribute to our behavior.[1]

The ABC model consists of three parts: A>B>C. However, in our everyday lives, many people only pay attention to two: A and C.

Antecedent: The trigger or event. It can be something

external, like a time, a place, or a person, or something internal, like a mood, a thought, or a feeling.

Consequence: The consequence of the event.

It's easy to believe that A causes C.

<u>Example 1</u>.

- *A* - Rahul plays video games until the early morning hours, even though he knows he needs more sleep and wants to log off before midnight.
- *C* - He feels like a failure when he realizes he has slept in again and is late for work. He is severely sleep-deprived and makes avoidable mistakes at work, putting his job at risk.

<u>Example 2</u>.

- *A* - Mary picks up a donut every afternoon on her 4:00 p.m. break despite wanting to cut out sugar, eat healthier, and lose some weight.
- *C* - She is frustrated and believes she has no self-control. She feels like she is never going to be able to lose weight and eventually gives up trying.

However, as we learned in Chapter 3, there is another factor at work in the habit loop:

Behavior: This is the key to making or breaking habits. There is space to choose your reaction to the trigger and build your desired habit. Understanding that we can take control of our response to triggers is key to breaking bad habits and creating good ones. Choosing an alternative behavior is possible.

It is not A that causes C but B.[2]

Let's look at the above examples again, but this time, adding a behavior that can positively change the outcome.

Antecedent>Behavior>Consequence

<u>Example 1</u>.

- *A* - Rahul plays video games with his friends nightly.
- *B* - He knows that he won't be able to stop playing on his own, so he sets a timer for 11:30 p.m. as a warning that he has 30 minutes left to play. Rahul uses the bedtime alarm function on his console to shut it off automatically at midnight.
- *C* - He gets more than six hours of sleep at night, and his job performance has improved.

<u>Example 2</u>.

- *A* - Mary's 4:00 p.m. break time comes, and she craves something to eat.
- *B* - During her 20-minute break, she unpacks the nutritious snack she brought from home and

enjoys it while walking around the block.

- *C* - Mary gets an energy boost from snacks. As she walks, she resists the temptation of the donut shop, reinforcing her dedication to healthy eating habits and weight loss efforts.

Many people successfully make positive changes by using the ABC model alone, but sometimes, digging deeper is necessary. Updated versions of the ABC model are more detailed, and D and E have been added.

D: Disputing an irrational belief to turn it into a rational one.

E: A new *Effect* as a consequence.

It is argued that D and E are already present in the original ABC model but have been made clearer in the expanded one. The expanded version shows how a change in thinking affects the outcome. In the expanded version, *B* is the original behavior that led to a negative outcome, and *D* leads to a more effective behavior, leading to *E*, a more positive effect.[2]

This more detailed method can help people break free of negative thought patterns by explicitly identifying and recognizing them, thenreplacing them with more neutral alternatives.

Example 1.

- *A* - Rahul misses his friends from home and has yet to make new friends in his new city, so he spends evenings playing online video games with his friends from home.

- *B* - He plays video games until the early morning hours, even though he knows he needs more sleep and wants to log off before midnight.
- *C* - He feels like a failure when he realizes he has slept in again and is late for work. He is severely sleep-deprived and makes avoidable mistakes at work, putting his job at risk.
- *D* - He realizes he is not a failure but lacks the self-control and discipline to turn off the video game on his own at a reasonable hour, so he comes up with another strategy. He knows that he won't be able to stop playing on his own, so he sets a timer for 11:30 p.m. as a warning that he has 30 minutes left to play. He uses the bedtime alarm function on his console to shut it off automatically at midnight.
- *E* - He gets more than six hours of sleep at night, and his job performance has improved.

Example 2.

- *A* - Mary is hungry every afternoon at 4:00 p.m., during her 20-minute break from work.
- *B* - Mary buys and eats a donut or two every afternoon despite wanting to cut out sugar and lose some weight.
- *C* - She is frustrated and believes she has no self-control. She feels like she is never going to be

able to lose weight and eventually gives up trying.

- *D* - Mary realizes that she buys donuts daily because she is hungry, it is convenient, and it has become a habit, not because she lacks self-control. She asks herself how she can change her donut habit while still enjoying an afternoon snack. She purchases a week's worth of healthy snacks and packs one for her 4:00 p.m. break daily as an alternative to buying donuts.
- *E* - Mary enjoys her nutritious snack from home and eats it on a walk around the block to avoid stopping at the donut shop.

The ABC(DE) Model works best when focused on one specific change at a time.

Identifying And Changing Negative Triggers

Triggers often result in people doing things that are unhealthy or unhelpful out of emotions like stress, boredom, anger, or loneliness. This can lead to bad habits, such as smoking, drinking, overeating, or gambling, ultimately harming their health, happiness, or productivity. However, bad habits don't always have to be so bad for us to still cause us harm. Being overly critical of ourselves or others, engaging in malicious gossip, talking badly about people behind their backs, or exhibiting excessively perfectionist tendencies are all bad habits that can affect our relationships and mental health.

A negative cue or trigger often results in avoidant behavior or behavior used as a coping mechanism. Procrastination is avoidant behavior. Biting your nails when anxious is a coping mechanism for your anxiety. Positive triggers, on the other hand, cause good feelings and associations with positive behaviors. For example:

- Runners often describe a "runners' high" that they experience after going for a run. The memory of that feeling helps motivate them to run again in the future.
- Placing a bowl of fruit on the kitchen counter or dining room table can make it more likely that you reach for fruit as a snack instead of something less nutritious.
- Wearing a fidget ring that you can twirl when anxious or nervous, to occupy your hands instead of reaching for a cigarette.
- Placing a book in the spot you drink your morning coffee or tea, to remind you to read for ten minutes each morning.

The ABC model above can help you identify your negative triggers and work through ways to turn them around, using strategies such as:

- *Avoiding* the negative trigger when possible
- *Reframing* by giving a different meaning to the triggering item, situation, or stimuli, or,

- *Replacing* or finding an alternative activity or location instead of the triggering one.

We will discuss some of these areas in more detail in Chapter 5, particularly how to arrange your environment to maximize positive triggers and minimize negative ones.

Creating And Using Positive Triggers

Some triggers can help us engage in positive habits that contribute to our well-being. These triggers help maintain good habits, like exercising, meditating, reading, or learning, which improve health, happiness, or productivity. Positive triggers can be created purposely by choosing obvious, relevant, and consistent ones. There are two tried-and-true techniques to help make positive habits easier to cultivate.

<u>Stacking</u>

Habit stacking involves adding a new behavior to an already ingrained habit. This makes it more likely that you will remember to engage in the new activity. There are some simple guidelines to follow to help improve the chances of success using this method:

1. Choose a habit that is simple to do, takes less than five minutes, and will improve your life in some way.
2. Attach it to an existing habit that makes logical sense. For example, make your bed immediately

after getting up in the morning or move $100 to a savings account as soon as you check your account balance on payday.

3. Make sure the new habit fits your life. If saving $100 is unrealistic based on your current financial situation, why not aim to save $50 or even $10? The idea is to get into the habit of putting money into your savings each payday before doing anything else with the cash. How much you actually save each pay can grow over time.[3]

<u>Pairing</u>

Pairing involves adding something you enjoy to a behavior you don't, making it more likely to continue with the activity you find less enjoyable. For example, perhaps you might choose to stream your favorite show while walking on the treadmill or listen to an audiobook while folding the laundry. It's even more effective if you can tie the enjoyable activity to the less enjoyable one.

Choosing The Best Rewards

Rewards are a big part of the habit loop, particularly when establishing new, good habits. Until a habit is entrenched in the brain and performed almost automatically, motivation in the form of a reward that makes a positive connection between the action and the outcome is helpful. As mentioned previously, one of the reasons good habits are so hard to start is because the reward is often delayed, making it more difficult to keep working toward it.

A reward doesn't have to be big or expensive but rather something that creates a positive association between action and outcome. Different types of rewards exist.

<u>Intrinsic Rewards</u>

These rewards are internal, such as feelings, thoughts, or memories of how a specific action makes you feel. These typically occur naturally and don't require much action on your part. If your spouse's face lights up when you bring them a cup of tea each morning, you probably won't need much encouragement to keep it up.

Studies show that intrinsic rewards in the form of intentions can help predict success when beginning a new activity, such as an exercise routine. They also indicate that the repetition-habit association for new behaviors can be strengthened with intrinsic motivation and pleasure.[4] Intrinsic rewards are considered ideal since the reward is generated from within.

<u>Extrinsic Rewards</u>

These are external and include material and social rewards, like attention, affirmation, and acceptance. Extrinsic rewards are often organized under three subcategories:

1. *Temptation Bundling*: Pairing an activity you enjoy with a habit, such as watching a show while

riding a stationary bike.

2. *Temptation Sequencing*: Making a specific reward contingent on completing the habit, such as only listening to your favorite audiobooks when out on a walk.

3. *Token Economy*: Delay gratification by earning points, or tokens, that add up to a bigger reward. For example, studying French 30 minutes a day counts as a token. When you earn 10 tokens, the equivalent of five hours of study, you will book yourself a massage.[5]

Extrinsic rewards often provide an incentive to get started on a habit that otherwise may seem too hard, boring, or unappealing. External motivation is prompted by the reward itself and may aid in habit formation through the engagement of dopamine systems. However, if extrinsic rewards are withdrawn, the motivation to continue the behavior can wane if the habit has not yet been completely formed.[6]

For rewards to be effective, they must be meaningful, satisfying, and aligned with your goals and values. If intrinsic rewards aren't strong enough, don't hesitate to choose something extrinsic that will be more effective. However, avoid rewards that are harmful, addictive, or counterproductive.

Action Steps

1. *Create your own ABC(DE) Model.*

This model works best for targeting one specific behavior change at a time. If Mary had tried to change ALL her negative eating patterns at once, it would have been too overwhelming to be effective. Instead, she focused first on the 4:00 p.m. snack. Name one bad habit you would like to change and focus on one specific behavior using the ABC(DE) Model as your guide.

2. *Stack or Pair.*

Which behaviors could you stack or pair with a new habit you want to cultivate? Choose two to try out this week.

3. *Choose your rewards.*

Decide which type of reward would be most effective for you and put it in place. Have an alternative in case it isn't strong enough.

Creating positive triggers and rewards helps encourage good habit formation. In Chapter 5, we'll explore our environment's role in our habits and learn how to manage our environment to support our habit goals.

Chapter Summary

- Triggers are neurophysical connections between cravings, feelings, and actions in connection to a situation or an experience.

- The ABC Model uses Antecedent, Behavior, and Consequence to analyze habits and make positive changes. More updated models also include D for Disputing an irrational belief and E for the new Effect.
- Creating a list of rewards can help keep habits on the right track. To be effective, rewards should be meaningful, satisfying, and aligned with our goals and values.
- Strategies like stacking or pairing can improve the chance of successfully adopting a new habit and can keep momentum.

PILLAR 4 - THE HABITAT OF GOOD HABITS

HOW YOUR SURROUNDING CAN BLOOM SUSTAINABLE HABITS FOR A HEALTHY WELL-BEING

I n Chapter 3, we read about Armindo's social smoking habit. Hanging out with friends and colleagues socially triggered his desire to smoke. In Armindo's case, the location wasn't a trigger as much as the people he was with. For others, elements of a physical location can have an influence, positive or negative, on their behavior.

Grace could never seem to get her work done on time. While everyone else was easily hitting deadlines, she struggled daily to complete her to-do list without taking work home each evening. She tried everything she could to improve her productivity, but nothing worked.

Grace arrived 30 minutes before everyone else so she could work without distractions. She closed her office door to work uninterrupted and changed to only checking her emails twice daily. She put her phone on Do Not Disturb and only checked it at lunch.

Yet, she still couldn't get her work done on time.

Grace lived alone, so she could work uninterrupted in the evenings, but she still struggled to be productive. She couldn't understand the problem. She loved her job and was good at what she did, but she just couldn't seem to concentrate the way she knew she should.

Desperate to complete a big project by the deadline, Grace rented a hotel room for the weekend for a change of pace. Upon arrival, she ordered room service, opened her computer, and got to work. Miraculously, she finished the project the first evening in record time and had the entire next day and evening to relax. She kept trying to figure out what was different about this weekend that improved her productivity. She was packing up her computer when it hit her.

The hotel room's desk was completely clear. There was no clutter, files, papers, agenda, calendar, or photos—just her computer and a glass of water. Grace pictured her desks at work and at home. They were the definition of cluttered. Files and papers were piled next to each other, a huge desk calendar sat under her computer, and various photos and knickknacks that brought her joy were lined up along the back.

Grace's environmental clutter was affecting her productivity. She spent Sunday afternoon clearing her desk at home and Monday morning clearing her desk at work. Following the cleaning spree, Grace's productivity jumped at work so much that over the next month, she didn't have to bring work home at all. Inspired by the improvement removing her desk clutter had on her work productivity, Grace embarked on a mission to declutter her home, starting with her bedroom. She realized how visual clutter affected her ability to function in different areas of life. She found she was able to improve many personal habits that she had struggled with as she removed the physical clutter from her environment.

We often think of habits as actions we perform regardless of where we are or who is around us, but the truth is that our environment is full of triggers. As we know, habits are responses to cues in our environment.[1] The fourth pillar of the habit mechanism is all about spaces—your room, workplace, social settings. This chapter will help you identify the environmental triggers affecting your long-term habits so you can make the right adjustments to support new habits. It will suggest what to do when changing the environment itself is not an option.

How The Environment Affects Lifelong Habits

Our environment can set the tone for a particular mindset, trigger associations, and feature specific negative triggers that affect our habits. The world around us influences our behavior, mood, and cognition. Factors such as colors, layout, temperature, lighting, and sounds can all impact how we feel and behave. Studies show that a cluttered room can increase cortisol levels, the stress hormone.[2] Just as we influence the world, we are also impacted by the world around us.

Imagine a crowded bus on a hot summer day. The bus is packed with people shoved up against each other. You can't find a seat, so you find yourself standing, trying not to lose your balance each time the bus comes to a stop. The windows are open, but there is no air conditioning, and your work attire is too hot for the temperature inside. Someone is eating what smells like a tuna sandwich, and the general stench of body odor is overwhelming. The ride to your stop is still another 30 minutes, and your feet already hurt in the new shoes pinching your feet all day.

How do you feel? When you get off the bus, will you be looking forward to going for a run, making a nutritious meal, or working on that report that's due tomorrow?

Now imagine yourself on that same bus on the way home from work. Only this time, the bus is nearly empty, the AC is working, and you have a seat next to an old friend from school that you were fortunate enough to run into unexpectedly. You spend the 30-minute ride catching up on old times and make plans to meet up for dinner on the weekend.

How do you feel? Would you be more or less likely to engage in some positive habits once you get off the bus in this scenario than the last?

Our environment includes more than just the specific room we are in at a particular time. In many ways, our environment can matter more than motivation when it comes to our habits.[3] We spend our days in multiple environments, which include people, objects, and even memories that can trigger us.

Keeping your cell phone charged on your nightstand can increase how often you check it at night, disrupting sleep. Having a TV or other screen in the bedroom can do the same. Using a timer for screens, removing them from the bedroom, or putting our cell phones on do-not-disturb mode overnight can encourage us to use the bedroom for rest and relaxation, not scrolling social media.

When we change the way we look at our environment, the relationship between environment and habits becomes clearer. Rather than thinking about our environment as filled with things, we should see it as filled with relationships.[3] A person living alone may see their dining room table as where they spend their evenings working on puzzles and eating their meals at the breakfast bar. That person's relationship to her dining room table is one of evening entertainment.

A young professional may rarely eat at home and only use their dining room table when they need to finish some work after hours. Their relationship to their dining room table is one of utility.

A couple with two children may use their dining room table for homework help, arts and crafts, and family dinners. Their relationship with their dining room table is the heart of their home.

Why Optimizing Your Environment Can Support Healthy Habits

Optimizing your environment is one of the best ways to support the adoption of different types of good habits. Making it easy to engage in a habit by optimizing the environment can increase the chances of success.[4] You may find that you have more control over certain environments, like your bedroom, than others, like your workplace, but try to work within the parameters of what's available. Let's compare what might be possible at home and in the office.

<u>Home</u>

Home is where you can arrange your environment to best support your habits, such as healthy eating, regular exercise, stress reduction, good sleep hygiene, and relaxation. Your home can either support those good habits or encourage bad ones. Some sample changes to support the cultivation of good habits might include:

1. *Physical Health Habits*: Keep your workout clothes laid out on a chair in your bedroom so they are ready for a workout first thing in the morning or right when you get home. A yoga mat in the corner of the bedroom rolled out and ready to use can encourage yoga practice. A fridge and pantry stocked with nutritious choices can encourage healthier eating habits. A bedroom painted in soothing colors with lowlights and soft bedding can encourage better sleep habits.

2. *Mental Health Habits*: The yoga mat in the corner of the bedroom can also serve as a meditation spot. A journal on your bedside table can be a place to start a gratitude practice. A quiet reading nook or a "calm down" spot with a comfortable spot to sit and headphones to block out noise can help you de-stress.

3. *Social habits*: Having an inviting space that you are proud of can encourage you to invite friends over regularly. Investing in cookware or dinnerware can make you feel proud to host friends or family gatherings.

Office

We typically have less control over our workspaces than our homes, but there are some areas over which we have some control.

1. *Physical Health Habits*: Wearing running shoes to and from work increases the likelihood of walking and taking the stairs or using them as an incentive to take a lunchtime walk. Bringing your lunch, rather than buying it at least a few days a week, can improve eating habits by taking control of the meal's nutritional value. If there is a gym in or near your place of work, heading there directly before or after work can help avoid the temptation to skip a workout.

2. *Mental Health Habits*: You may not be able to control who your manager is or your colleagues' personalities, but you can try to protect your peace at work.

Perhaps the noise of the office makes it hard to concentrate. If appropriate, consider headphones, closing your office door, or seeking out an empty conference room from time to time.

Perhaps your work environment is negative due to office politics. To keep yourself removed from those conversations, avoid office gossip and keep conversations light and generic.

If you work in a fast-paced environment that is highly stressful and causes you to feel overwhelmed, practice mindful breathing techniques that can be done at any time, such as taking four slow, deep breaths in through your nose and out through your mouth.

3. *Social Habits*: Socializing at work is a personal choice, but it can make the day go by more quickly if you have at least one colleague you enjoy working with. Keep personal conversations to a minimum during the workday. When attending work social events, consider them to be work and behave accordingly. Limit consumption of alcoholic beverages and behave in a way that reflects your position. Work social events can be a great way to network with other departments and make connections that may serve you later in your career.

<u>General Considerations When Optimizing An Environment</u>

1. *Removing Distractions*. Minimizing clutter, noise, or electronic devices can help improve focus when working or allow for deeper relaxation when trying to sleep.

2. *Adding Positive Cues.* These can remind or inspire you to think about performing a good habit. For example, a notebook on your bedside table can remind you to journal, or a gratitude jar on the counter in the kitchen can remind you to write down and add what you are grateful for every morning before making breakfast.

3. *Creating Specific Zones.* Even in tiny spaces, it is important to try and set up different zones for different activities. Keeping the bedroom for sleeping and not working can improve sleep quality. If you live in a studio apartment where everything happens in one small space, divide it as much as possible. For example, use a small desk for working, and keep your bed for sleeping only. Eat at a table, and perhaps have a small corner with a chair for reading or relaxing.

Coping With Environmental Factors You Can't Control

Despite your best efforts, there will be times when you won't be able to control the environment in a way that is conducive to your needs. You might have noisy roommates who keep the house full of clutter, or your family might not want to make the same dietary changes that you do, and you may be confronted with a pantry full of snacks you are trying to avoid.

It won't always be possible to adjust to the environment, but you can, instead, adjust your behavior and work toward the type of compromise that is good for everyone.

1. <u>Communication</u>

Express your goals to friends, family, or coworkers. If your goal is to respond to emails within a 48-hour window, be honest about it and outline what that might mean in terms of your behavior at work.

Many people find it hard to say 'no' to other people's requests or offers, especially if it's for fun activities, even if they run counter to the habits you're trying to cultivate. Telling your friends that you're cutting back on alcohol and would prefer to meet up where beer is not sold can help them understand when you turn down offers to go out and can help create new options for hanging out.

2. Set Boundaries

If your new bedtime is 11:00 p.m., then you must turn down all offers to go out or stay up past that time. Letting people know about your boundary is the first step to making it stick. If other people in your home want to stay up later than that, invest in a sleep mask and noise-canceling headphones to stick to your goal without being annoyed by others.

3. Negotiation

If your new habits are inconveniencing others, compromise to create a win-win solution for everyone. Sometimes, when we radically change our behavior, it can conflict with the relationships we have built with other people. If those relationships are important to us, such as with a spouse or close friend, then we must learn to compromise in a way that allows us to keep our new habits while still respecting their impact on other people.

Choosing to train for a triathlon will impact the amount of time you have for your spouse and children. What kinds of compromises need to happen so that your spouse doesn't end up shouldering more than their share of the housework and childcare so that you can reach your goal?

4. Adaptation

In a perfect world, the circumstances around the habits we want to adopt would be optimal. The weather would always be just right. There would be no unpleasant life surprises, health scares, or financial constraints. Unfortunately, we are imperfect people living in an imperfect world, so learning to adapt to less-than-perfect circumstances is a must. Sometimes, that means scaling down our expectations or rethinking how we perform a habit. If your mornings are crazy with small children and a terrible commute, an elaborate morning meditation and exercise routine probably isn't realistic. Perhaps a ten-minute meditation right after getting out of bed and then an evening workout after the kids go to bed is more achievable.

Consider A Change Of Location

Sometimes, it's easier to break a habit or cultivate a new one by changing the environment altogether. If we are tempted to drink, eat, or spend too much in certain places, avoiding them entirely while we break those habits may be necessary. However, it can also be useful to frequent certain places when we want to create new habits. This is known as "disrupting the context."[5]

If working or studying at home is not easy due to the environment, consider a library or coworking space instead. If office gossip has become overwhelming and puts you in a bad mood, avoid the break room and eat your lunch elsewhere. If running alone isn't happening, join a running group and head to a local parkrun on Saturday mornings.

Action Steps

1. *Assess your environment.*

Take a proactive approach to understanding how your surroundings influence your habits. Identify areas of your environment that may be triggering negative behaviors or hindering your ability to engage in healthy habits.

2. *Remove distractions.*

Identify and eliminate distractions in your environment that may be impeding your focus or productivity. Take steps to create a conducive environment for concentration and task completion.

3. *Add positive cues.*

Intentionally incorporate positive cues into your environment to prompt and inspire healthy habits.

Understanding environmental triggers and reorganizing our environments to support positive habits sets us up for success in many areas. Chapter 6 is where we begin to put it all together and commit to making our new healthy habits last for the long term.

Chapter Summary

- Our environment helps shape who we are and how we behave.
- Consider an environment as being filled with relationships rather than objects.
- Rearrange your environment to be less conducive to negative habits and more conducive to positive ones.
- Consider a change of environment when trying to adopt certain new habits.

6

PILLAR 5 - STICKING LIKE HONEY

HOW TO MAKE NEW POSITIVE HABITS SO SWEET THAT YOU DON'T WANT TO LET GO

Patrick always liked to start new habits but could never make them stick. As a teenager, he took up guitar but often slept in and missed his Saturday lessons. He didn't set up a regular practice time and eventually would leave his guitar untouched for months. In college, he signed up for German lessons, a language he had always wanted to learn but preferred hanging at the pub with his friends to sitting in a classroom on Thursday evenings. He stopped attending his language class before the semester was through. In his late twenties, he enrolled in a martial arts class, but showing up to class three days a week proved difficult, as something always seemed to come up, so he quit three months later.

His thirties panned out much the same way. Patrick would start something new that he hoped to make a habit out of, but inevitably something would get in the way and he would quit before the habit took off. On his 40th birthday, he made a vow to himself that he would turn this tendency around in his 40s.

Rather than jump right into the next thing that caught his attention, Patrick took some time to identify the most important habits he wanted to develop. Then, he chose just two to focus on one new habit at a time over the course of the year. He first decided to take up martial arts again. He had always regretted not making it past the first belt and worried that if he didn't start now, he might never go back. He also thought it was a good way to incorporate regular exercise into his week.

Patrick thought back on his last experience and knew he needed to approach it differently this time. He started by choosing a program that had classes only one day per week at a time that allowed him to head to class directly from work. He then added the class to his calendar and set up an alarm to remind him. He kept a bag with his uniform in his car so he wouldn't forget it.

Though Patrick didn't work late often, he knew that there was a possibility that it could happen occasionally. He chose a martial arts school that allowed make-up classes during any of the other scheduled class times. Patrick used that as his backup plan, thinking, "If I can't make my regular class, then I will attend a make-up class the same week." He knew that he needed to be flexible and be able to adapt to changing circumstances to keep up the habit of attending.

In the past, his goal had been to become a black belt, and he hadn't even made it to the first belt change. This time, his goal was to practice martial arts a minimum of once a week to improve his strength, flexibility, and discipline.

Building and maintaining positive habits isn't always easy. It's essential to plan not just for the easy days but also for those days when sticking to a new habit seems almost impossible. Planning ensures overviewing our entire situation, including the habits that we wish to form, the difficulties we'll face, and a plan to overcome obstacles.

The Expanded Habit Loop

At the beginning of the book, the formula for habit formation was presented as Cue > Behavior > Reward. The *cue* triggers the behavior or the habit. The *behavior* is the habit. Finally, the *reward* is what the habit gives you that makes it addictive. We later looked at how the cue can set off a range of reactions, including *Behavior, Emotions, Sensations, and Thoughts (BEST)*, and that taking the time to understand those reactions to the cue could help give us the space we need to change the habit that forms as a result.

In this pillar, we are going to dig even deeper and add another dimension to the habit loop. In James Clear's book *Atomic Habits*, he presents the habit loop as having four components.[1]

Cue > Craving > Response (Behavior) > Reward

Cue

We already know that this is the trigger. In bad habits, the cue is often invisible or at least not intentional. We may not realize that the stress of our clutter is causing us to procrastinate, but the cue is there. In good habits, the key is to make the cue visible or obvious. We can continue to perform a habit without identifying the cue, but we cannot change a habit without knowing what the cue is and changing it to suit the new habit we want to develop. If you want to develop the habit of making your bed every day, the cue should be getting up. As soon as you get out of bed, you should make it immediately.

Craving

This is our desire to engage in the behavior that creates the habit. In bad habits, the craving is often for the temporary good feeling that comes at the expense of long-term harm. The feeling one gets immediately after smoking a cigarette is immediate, and as such, often wins out over the long-term harm and increased cancer risk of a smoking habit.

Since good habits are often ones with delayed satisfaction, it can be more complicated to create the craving in the early stages of habit formation. Associating the new habit with something positive can be helpful. A morning walk can be more enjoyable when accompanied by a friend or when it's taken along a scenic route.

Response/Behavior

The key to doing the behavior is to make it easy to engage in. When breaking an old habit, a replacement behavior is necessary to achieve the outcome you desire.[2] Making that behavior as easy to engage in as the one that is being replaced increases your chances of success. Change is always hard, and changing from something easy to achieve with immediate payoff to something hard to achieve with delayed gratification makes things harder than they need to be.

If you have a habit of biting your nails and want to stop, having a piece of gum or something else to chew on instead available whenever you get the urge will be more likely to help you break the habit than willpower alone. Likewise, if checking your phone first thing in the morning is a habit you would like to break, moving your phone from your bedroom may be helpful, but you still need something to fill that void. Otherwise, you will just get up and get the phone. Having a journal by your bed, listening to a morning podcast, or doing 10 minutes of stretching first thing can help replace the old behavior and distract your mind from craving it.

Reward

The reward must be satisfying, particularly in the early stages of habit formation, when gratification is often delayed. Having a well-thought-out reward can help while the habit is being developed. Consider rewards that will reinforce or take you deeper into the habit. If your goal is to add weight training to your fitness routine three days a week, rewarding yourself with new training gloves, a set of dumbbells, or something else related to the activity is one way to reinforce the habit and reward yourself for sticking to the plan. In the nail-biting example above, treating yourself to a manicure after a week of not biting your nails is a logical reward for committing to the habit for seven days.[1]

Enhance Your Chance Of Success

Starting and sticking with new habits is hard, but there are ways to make it more fun and easier. Habits stick better when they are one or more of the following.

1. <u>Obvious</u>. An obvious cue that serves as a clear reminder can take the guesswork out. Consider using a wall calendar, a sticky note, or a phone notification to remind you. Stacking new habits to already entrenched ones, like drinking a whole glass of water at each meal, can make it easy to remember and logical to apply.

2. <u>Attractive</u>. This makes you *want* to keep up the habit, such as a reward, an incentive, or a positive association. We talked about how to choose the best incentives and rewards for you in Chapter 5.

3. <u>Easy</u>. Sticking to new habits is more likely when we make it easier, such as implementing a routine, a shortcut, or a simplification. Choosing to repeat an action at the same time every day is an example. Sarah Coomer advocates for "micro dosing wellness" by adding small habits to our day that make our lives better.[3] Don't have

time to practice yoga for 30 minutes? Try a 10-minute practice. Need a mood boost at 3 p.m. most days but are stuck in the office? Take a five-minute bathroom break and listen to one great song in your headphones before returning to your desk.

4. <u>Satisfying</u>. Each time you finish performing the habit, it's important that it brings some sort of satisfaction. This is why many habit-forming applications offer immediate feedback or praise in some form to give that boost of satisfaction for things that may take time for big results to become obvious.

Don't Let Obstacles Get You Down

Everyone faces some challenges that make it harder to stick to their habits. We all feel lazy, get distracted, or are tempted by the wrong things from time to time. Obstacles to success come in different forms but often share the same qualities. Remember, habit formation is not linear.[4]

One of the most effective changes you can make is to focus on your *systems* instead of just one particular goal. That may sound counterproductive, but it's not. This doesn't mean you shouldn't set any goals for yourself. It simply means that each goal is just one part of the *bigger process*. If your goal is to read 52 books over the course of the year and you only read 50, objectively, you will have failed.

However, if you only read two books the previous year, it's hard for anyone to see an improvement of an extra 48 books read as a failure. If you spend your year focusing on the systems approach to making reading a daily part of your life, whether you read 40, 50, or the actual 52 books, you have picked up a habit that will last long after you hit that magical number. By focusing on the systems approach to reading, incorporating a little bit of reading every day is a success since the big picture habit is to become a reader, not finish reading an arbitrary number of books.

Choose Lifelong Areas Of Improvement Over Temporary Goals

When building habits, goals are better seen as milestones on a lifelong journey. Otherwise, your habit has a very defined beginning and end point. Rather than choosing a finite goal, consider choosing to build habits in one of the 10 most common areas of improvement: Time, Sleep, Food, Fitness, Space, Play, People, Money, Spirit, or Voice.[3]

1. *Time*: Making time for the things that are important to you is a habit in itself! Where can you fit in one minute of deep breathing or mindfulness? How can you find five minutes to stretch? When can you take twenty minutes to practice that new hobby?

2. *Sleep*: An alarming number of people are sleep deprived, either from not enough or poor quality sleep. In the United States, nearly 1 in 3 adults report not getting enough sleep daily, and an estimated 50 to 70 million have a chronic sleep disorder.[5] What would help improve

yours? A regular bedtime? A calm-down routine in the evening? A more comfortable sleeping environment? A regular wake-up time?

3. *Food*: Building a healthy relationship with food is not about dieting but about creating healthy eating habits that will last a lifetime. Where would you like to improve your habits? Eating regular meals? Eating a wider variety of foods? Learning to be a better cook so you can cook daily?

4. *Fitness*: Fitness habits are not just about losing weight or building big muscles. What would better fitness look like for you? Being a regular runner? Practicing functional fitness to age more strongly? Moving 30 minutes a day?

5. *Space*: This refers specifically to the physical environments in which you spend your time. How do you feel in the different rooms in your home? Does the clutter make you anxious? Is there something you have been meaning to fix, and it makes you feel guilty for not having done so every time you walk by it? Space habits can be figuring out how to incorporate daily chores into your schedule, a monthly "fix it" schedule, or anything that helps you feel more at ease in the places where you spend your time.

6. *Play*: How often do you play? Is your life filled with what seems like endless obligations? What would adding more play look like for you? Weekly game night with the family? Learning a new sport or hobby?

7. *People*: Isn't it strange how we often struggle to make a habit of spending time with the people who mean the most to us? There is a loneliness epidemic in the United States, where life has gotten in the way of nurturing those relationships that keep us happy and fulfilled. What would building a "people" habit include? Weekly phone calls to parents or siblings who live far away? A monthly dinner with friends? Joining a community group to meet new people?

8. *Money*: Many of us struggle with our money habits but never quite seem to get a grip on which area to attend to first. Should you set up an automatic savings habit? A monthly spending limit? Return to using cash only for daily expenses?

9. *Spirit*: Nurturing your spirit can mean different things to different people. Would you like to reconnect with your faith? Perhaps become more spiritual in the sense of connecting with the universe or engaging in mindfulness? Or perhaps by spirit, you simply want to engage in the type of things that simply make your spirit happy?

10. *Voice*: This is about how comfortable you are being yourself, expressing your opinions, and using your voice. Do you find yourself changing who you are or how you behave around certain people? Do you wish you could speak your truth more often? What changes do you need to make to live more authentically and project your true self to the world?[3]

Implementation Intentions, Better Known As If-Then Plans

If-Then plans have been shown to be successful in helping to turn intention into action. They work like this: "*If* X happens, *then* I will do Y." More specifically, if *situation*, then *habit*. It turns vague intentions into clear, actionable habits.[6]

Some examples might include, I want to eat healthier. This might become: If I eat dinner at a restaurant, then I will order a green vegetable and a side salad with my meal. Or, I want to stop yelling at my children when I'm angry. The if-then plan might be, If I feel like yelling at my children, then I will take a five-minute break to cool down before talking to them calmly.

If-then plans are helpful in that they explicitly set out the behavior to be performed in a specific set of often challenging circumstances. It is like creating an algorithm for your habits. However, it is important to note that these plans can also be fairly rigid and may not always provide the flexibility you need in every situation.

Pre-Commitments, Or The Don't Let Me Do That! Model

This model is typically employed to overcome impulsivity. It is often used to take away an option that you would typically choose if available. It is essentially the act of restricting your own future choices so as to prioritize the outcome you want. It can be expressed as, "I will do X, so I won't do Y."

In this model, you are taking away, or restricting, the need to rely on willpower when making a choice about what behavior to engage in. You are preemptively taking away an option from your future self based on your current preferences. This happens by taking away access to temptations. It helps choose the option that often leads to delayed gratification.[7]

For example, the pre-commitment model you might employ if you want to start saving more money for retirement could be, *I will* have 10% of my pay automatically moved to a savings account *so I won't* spend it all. If your goal is to be more present with your significant other but find yourself glued to your phone each night instead, it might look like, *I will* set my phone to Do Not Disturb after 7 p.m. *so I won't* use it in the evenings.

Backup Plans

A backup plan for habit formation works much like those in any area of life. It provides an alternative or option that keeps up the habit, even when something goes wrong. When creating a backup plan, it's important to acknowledge that while the backup behavior might not be the exact habit behavior you had planned for, it is enough to keep the habit momentum going. It allows for flexibility and a "something is better than nothing" mindset. This looks like, "If I can't do X, then I will do Y."

Perhaps your plan is to head to the gym after work each night, but you get stuck at work too late to go several nights this week due to a big project deadline. Your backup plan could be, "*If I can't* go to the gym, *then I will* do an at-home workout instead." The key is to choose an alternative that keeps the momentum going until you can return to the original plan or make a new one if necessary.

Be Flexible And Adaptable

Flexibility: 1. The ability to change to suit new conditions or situations. 2. The ability to bend easily without breaking. While the second definition is meant to apply to objects, it is fair to apply it more figuratively as well.[8]

Adaptability: Being able to change or be changed in order to deal successfully with new situations. To be adaptable means that you can adjust to changing circumstances, learn from experience, and change course accordingly.[9]

You'll notice that the *Oxford English Dictionary's* definitions of flexibility and adaptability are almost identical. However, there are some generally accepted differences between the two. Flexibility is often referred to as the ability to react quickly in an unexpected or immediate situation, while adaptability often refers to being able to adjust to an anticipated change.

For the purposes of habit formation, we'll use this distinction when discussing how flexibility and adaptability can help with making and keeping new positive habits.

No matter how well we lay out our plans for a new behavior, life doesn't always go to plan. Being flexible in our habits means that when something pops up unexpectedly that gets in the way of our scheduled habit, we are able to work around it. A flat tire may cause you to miss your dance class this week, but you can still go home and practice the moves you learned last week to keep up the weekly dancing habit. Illness, injury, or unexpected emergencies or situations out of our control require flexibility with our habits.

Adaptability, in this sense, relates more to long-term change, when we permanently change what, how, or when we do things. Changing seasons may affect where you get in your workout, particularly if your workout of choice is seasonal in nature. Moving to a new city or getting a new job with a longer commute could mean that some location-specific habits will have to be adapted (e.g., finding a new location). Moving in with someone, starting a family, or even age-related changes can mean being adaptable so that your habits can change with you.

Action Steps

1. Choose one habit you are trying to develop. How can you make it easier?

List at least one way you can make it more:

- a. Obvious:
- b. Attractive:

- c. Easy:
- d. Satisfying:

2. *Most habits fall under one of the following 10 categories: Time, Sleep, Food, Fitness, Space, Play, People, Money, Spirit, or Voice.*

Think about some of the habits you are working on building. Have you been thinking about them in terms of fixed goals or lifestyle changes? Turn your goals into lifelong habits by first identifying where they fit into the above categories.

Mastering your habits means planning for success and being able to handle the changes that life throws at you. The fifth pillar is all about making habits appealing so they stick. Essentially, it's building habits that withstand time! To do this successfully, finding a support system and accessing the right resources are key. Chapter 7 will help you decide which outside resources are best for your personal habit journey.

Chapter Summary

- The Habit Loop adds an extra dimension to habit formation. The loop is Cue > Craving > Response (Behavior) > Reward.
- Making a new habit more appealing to stick with involves making it Obvious, Attractive, Easy, or Satisfying.
- Focusing on systems rather than goals is better for long-term habit formation. Instead, build

habits around one or more of the 10 most common areas of improvement: Time, Sleep, Food, Fitness, Space, Play, People, Money, Spirit, or Voice.

- Flexibility and adaptability are key, as life changes in unexpected ways.

PILLAR 6 - NOT ALONE

FIND YOUR TRIBE, FUEL YOUR PASSION, AND
FORGE A PATH TO SUSTAINABLE HABITS FOR
LASTING CHANGE TOGETHER

David was a 33-year-old single professional having difficulty managing his finances. Despite his best efforts, David constantly overspent and lived beyond his means. He impulsively bought things he didn't need, ate out frequently, took expensive vacations, and neglected to track his expenses. This all led to mounting credit card debt and financial stress. Not to mention that he still owed a significant amount of student loan debt. David wanted to buy his own condo and stop leasing his vehicle, but he couldn't scrape together a down payment, and his bad credit rating made it difficult for him to secure a mortgage or loan.

As David's debt grew, he realized that he needed to make a change. However, he felt overwhelmed and unsure of where to start. He lacked the knowledge and support system necessary to take control of his finances and make responsible decisions about money management. David discovered a financial literacy workshop aimed at young professionals like himself offered by a local university. Intrigued by the opportunity to learn more about personal finance, he decided to attend the workshop and see what it had to offer.

At the workshop, David was introduced to the basic principles of budgeting, saving, and debt management. He learned practical strategies for creating a budget, tracking expenses, and setting financial goals. He also gained insight into the importance of building an emergency fund and saving for the future. At the end of the workshop, attendees were offered the opportunity to join a free financial recovery support group with monthly accountability meetings and an online chat group to provide ongoing mutual support.

David signed up and attended his first meeting the following week, where he was both shocked and relieved to discover that a significant number of members were around the same age and in a similar financial situation. Rather than feeling judged, he felt seen and understood. Inspired by what he had learned, David decided to take action and implement some of the strategies he had picked up at the workshop and the support group.

He created a monthly budget outlining his income and expenses, prioritizing essentials like rent, groceries, and utilities while setting aside money for savings and debt repayment. The financial accountability group helped keep him accountable. They shared progress, offered support, and held each other accountable for sticking to their financial goals.

With the guidance of the workshop facilitators and the support of his accountability group, David began to see positive changes in his financial habits. He became more mindful of his spending, cutting back on nonessential expenses and finding ways to save money. He also developed a plan for paying off his credit card debt, making regular payments, and avoiding new charges. He felt a sense of empowerment and control over his finances that he had never experienced before.

A year later, David had significantly decreased his debt, was turning his credit score around, and had implemented a savings plan for a down payment on a condo. He had attended additional financial security workshops and continued to participate faithfully in the accountability group. Rather than feeling overwhelmed and out of control with his money, David feels confident in his ability to manage his finances and achieve his financial goals.

Breaking bad habits and starting good ones can feel like a lonely, solitary exercise, but it doesn't have to be. Seeking out a support system of people can provide a community of support, and employing the use of resources to help keep you on track can increase your chances of success—and this is the sixth pillar of habit building.

Why Support And Resources Matter

How often have you tried to do something difficult all on your own, only to realize you were making things much harder on yourself than necessary? For example, research shows that peer support groups are particularly effective in individuals achieving weight loss success, whether the groups provide in-person or online support.[1] Programs such as Alcoholics Anonymous and Weight Watchers have provided support for individuals looking for a community to help them stay sober or lose weight for decades.

Breaking bad habits and starting good habits can be an overwhelming endeavor. Trying to do it alone can be too much to handle. There are several areas in which breaking or making a habit can be more difficult without the right resources and support.

1. <u>Accountability</u>: We aren't all great at keeping ourselves accountable. It's easy to cheat, skip steps, or convince ourselves that we are doing better than we are without an objective person or system in place to keep us accountable.

2. <u>Overwhelm</u>: Breaking bad habits, especially long-entrenched ones, can be intimidating. Starting a new habit can be equally scary. Sometimes, that overwhelm is enough to stop us from even trying. Having someone by your side to help can make it all seem more manageable.

3. <u>Isolation</u>: It can be lonely facing down new challenges alone, particularly if the new habit you are trying to

cultivate takes you to places you find intimidating, like joining a gym, taking a new class, or showing up somewhere new alone.

4. Discouragement: Setbacks, failures, and hard days can lead to discouragement. It can be hard to break out of that feeling alone, leading to slow or even no progress on habit-breaking or new habit formation.

Support Systems

Support systems are commonly considered when trying to break a bad habit but should not be overlooked when developing a new one. A support system is a person or group of people whose role is to provide guidance, feedback, encouragement, accountability, or companionship on your journey. A support system can include friends, family, medical experts, therapists, mentors, teachers, coaches, or anyone who helps you achieve your goals.

How Can Support Systems Help

Think of your support system as a community. It could be a community of two—you and another person—or a bigger community, but regardless of how many people it contains, it should feel like a true community. If you don't feel like your support system is making you feel and behave better, then it's not right for you.

Some benefits of a support system include:

1. *Accountability*: Having someone else to answer to can be enough to keep us on track, whether it's a workout partner, coach, or even just a family member who checks in weekly. Accountability is more than just sharing our goals with another person; it's knowing that the person is going to be checking in and holding us to it that makes the difference.

Ideally, an accountability partner or group will ask us the hard questions when we aren't keeping up with our habits, challenging our excuses, and offering suggestions for progress. They are not just there to commiserate when things don't go according to plan; they are there to encourage us to keep going and challenge us to improve. Individuals are more likely to take advice and guidance from those they feel connected to.[2]

2. *Motivation/Discipline*: As mentioned in the earlier chapter, motivation isn't always easy to sustain, which is why the discipline of showing up even when we don't want to is a better formula for success. This can be supercharged by having an accountability partner, therapist, or mentor to keep us accountable.

Working out, studying, or pursuing any habit alongside others in which results can be measured can lead to greater motivation, including coming from a fear of missing out. If your cycling group meets up every Saturday morning for 60 km bike rides by the coast, it will be harder to keep up if your attendance is inconsistent. Seeing your group members progress will hopefully encourage you to want to progress alongside them and continue to be a member of the group.

3. *Shared Interests*: There is research that shows that we are more likely to adopt at least some of the behaviors of the people we spend the most time with, so choosing to spend our time with those whose habits or lifestyles we wish to emulate can help those good habits rub off on us! The social proximity effect is the term used to explain how we are more likely to engage in behaviors similar to those we spend the most time with. This includes both positive and negative behaviors.[3]

If your friends spend Friday and Saturday nights at pubs, sleeping in until noon on Sundays, chances are that you will adopt at least some of those behaviors, too. This would make it more difficult for you to join that Saturday morning parkrun group or a Sunday morning cooking class. When we surround ourselves with those who are pursuing some of the same habits we are, it is easier to incorporate them into our lives as well because there is less of a disconnect.

4. *Positive Reinforcement*: Whether it's a family member, friend, or professional, having someone to keep us in a positive mindset on those hard days can help keep us moving forward even when we don't want to!

We can, of course, provide ourselves with positive reinforcement, but that becomes easier the longer we have been engaging in the habit. In the early stages, when we feel unsure or out of place, someone who can help us keep our heads up can be the difference between pushing through our doubt or giving up before we give the habit a chance.

5. *Teaching and Advice*: We don't always know how to do everything or how to do things in the most effective manner. Hiring a coach, mentor, or therapist can be an invaluable resource.

First, they can help us start out on the right foot, helping us to avoid common errors or pitfalls that plague many beginners in any habit. Second, particularly for skilled habits, they can help avoid things like injury or incorrect form, essentially helping us to avoid developing bad habits within the good habit we are trying to cultivate!

Learning the right way to do something from the start can save you a lot of time and effort over the long run. It can also help see results more quickly. Not to mention that your coach or trainer can double as an accountability partner and a source of positive reinforcement. Coaching, in general, is associated with improvements in physical, mental, and emotional well-being.[4]

Participants in Alcoholics Anonymous or similar programs, for example, have a sponsor they can reach out to when they need support during their journey to sobriety, ensuring they don't feel alone. Some find mentors in their workplace or field to help them grow professionally. Every professional athlete has a team of coaches, trainers, and therapists to support them both physically and mentally during training. Support systems help keep us honest, focused, and committed to making lasting changes.

<u>Types Of Support Systems And How To Find Them</u>

1. *Informal*: This generally involves people you know, such as family, friends, colleagues, or acquaintances.

Pros: Informal support systems are usually free, so money is not an obstacle. Since you already know these people, you can get started feeling comfortable with them and skip the "getting to know you" stage before jumping right into leaning on them for support. These people are often already invested in their relationship with you and want to see you do well.

Cons: Free also means that their consistency and dedication are completely reliant on their personal level of dedication and reliability. It can be awkward to break off ties with someone you are close to if you no longer feel the arrangement is helpful. This type of support is often limited to emotional encouragement, motivation, and positive reinforcement, so if you need more professional or technical assistance, you may need to look elsewhere.

2. *Semi-formal/semi-professional*: These are support systems generally comprised of strangers in a more formally organized setting. This can include community groups such as Alcoholics Anonymous, runners' groups, or even

classes or programs that revolve around targeted areas of improvement (e.g., skills, health, productivity, etc.). These groups can be in-person or online, paid or free.

Pros: Can provide more specific, structured support from and alongside like-minded individuals with similar goals. They can focus on more than just the emotional and encouragement aspect of habit formation, by providing problem-solving, advice, and skills instruction.

Cons: Group settings and online forums or classes can be hit-or-miss in terms of quality and composition. A runners' group that isn't inclusive or doesn't make provisions for every runner can be more discouraging than encouraging for a very slow runner who can't keep up. As many of these types of support programs are often free or very low-cost, they do not always offer the type of dedicated one-on-one support you may be looking for.

3. *Formal/Professional*: This type of support system involves paying a professional for their time and energy. Coaches, doctors, therapists, teachers, and trainers fall into this category. They can work with you one-on-one, in a group setting, in person, or online. However, to really be a support, they must interact with you. Recorded classes that are one-way only fall under resources rather than support.

Pros: Expert, professional care and advice. Programs can be personalized and the advice is backed by the person's expert knowledge. They will generally be dedicated and consistent because it is a professional relationship.

Cons: This type of assistance and support can get expensive. Also, despite the "personal" touch, the relationship itself is professional, so certain boundaries shouldn't be crossed. It can be time-consuming and complicated to replace a professional at times.

Resources

In contrast to a support system, resources are the tools or materials that provide information, inspiration, education, and useful instructions for forming and maintaining habits. Resources can be specific to the habit you are trying to form or geared to habit formation and maintenance in general.

Books: A tried and true way to self-learn, and are resources you can return to again and again.

Websites: A great way to access information in a visual format from anywhere. YouTube has tutorials on almost every topic possible. LifeHack and ZenHabits are two sites that are specific to habits, and sites like Coursera offer courses so you can learn whatever you want.[5]

Podcasts: There are great podcasts out there that can keep you motivated or teach you something new. The Habit Podcast and Life Habits are two popular ones (Player FM).

Courses: In this case, pre-recorded or self-study courses can give you the information you need in a format that you can access or return to at any time.

<u>Vision boards</u>: These can be physical vision boards that you keep in a prominent place or can be created online via an app or a program. Vision boards keep you focused on your goals and can be great motivators when things get tough.

Guidance And Feedback

Your support system and the resources you choose to employ can be good sources of guidance and feedback, whether self-directed or as part of a larger group, helping you stay away from temptation while providing constructive criticism.

Support systems and tools can also help guard against perfectionism, which can lead to procrastination or paralysis. Perfectionists often lose motivation to perform an activity if they feel like they can't do it exactly as they imagined. Feedback helps build resilience and keep track of progress, helping you to see the gains you are making and encouraging you to keep going.

Action Steps

1. *Find Support.*

Choose one habit that you have been trying to accomplish alone but that could go more smoothly with a support system. Identify one person/group you could reach out to for each type of support, and commit to securing support in at least one of the three levels this month:

- Informal/Personal:
- Semi-Formal:
- Formal/Professional:

2. *Choose Resources.*

Sticking with the same habit in number one, make a list of resources that could help you meet this goal. Commit to employing two resources this month to build this habit.

Working on habits is less daunting when you have a support system in place and the right resources to provide you with the information you need to keep on track. In Chapter 8, we will delve deeper into how to use these and other resources to track your progress so you can hold yourself accountable over the long term.

Chapter Summary

- Trying to incorporate new habits alone without support can make them harder to stick to.
- Support systems provide guidance, feedback, encouragement, accountability, or companionship.
- Support systems can be informal/personal, such as friends and family; semi-formal, such as community groups; or formal/professional, such as therapists and coaches.

- Resources are tools or materials like books, apps, websites, podcasts, videos, or courses that provide information, inspiration, education, and useful instructions for forming and maintaining habits.
- Guidance and Feedback are essential for habit-building.

PILLAR 7 - THE HABIT-TRACKING KIT

HOW TO CHART YOUR COURSE TO SUCCESS
THROUGH HABIT-TRACKING WITH TOOLS AND
STRATEGIES TO MAP YOUR PROGRESS

Victor is a dedicated senior software engineer driven by his ambition to excel in his career. He is meticulous in his work, constantly striving for perfection, and rarely taking time to reflect on his progress. He often finds himself immersed in coding projects, losing track of time, and neglecting other aspects of his life. Victor's medium-term goal is to become a team manager, but he first needs to get promoted to tech lead and gain some additional experience. He has been recommended to look for a mentor to help him focus his efforts, but he never seems to find the time to reach out.

For years, Victor has poured his heart and soul into his work, pushing himself to the limit to meet deadlines and deliver flawless results. However, despite his efforts, he often feels he is falling short of his expectations. He agonizes over minor mistakes, berating himself for not being good enough. Twice in the past year, tech lead positions have popped up on his radar, but he hadn't felt secure enough in his abilities to apply. Instead, he watched as junior colleagues snapped up the spots, realizing too late that he should have taken the chance.

Victor failed to realize that his dedication and hard work were gradually paying off. His skills improved with each project, and he gained recognition within his company for his contributions. However, he was so focused on his perceived failures that he failed to acknowledge his growth and instead was waiting for the annual employee evaluation process to roll around for feedback. Only then would he be convinced that he is ready to take the next step on his career path. Unfortunately, evaluations were more than six months out, so he had a long wait ahead.

One morning, Victor's manager, Shaun, called him into his office. He had spent the weekend looking over a recent project and was impressed with what he saw. He knew Victor was a hard worker, but his shy, unassuming demeanor meant he never demanded recognition for his work. He was happy with a job well done. Shaun complimented Victor on the project and asked him why he was still in a senior engineer role rather than a tech lead or team leader. He told him that he had a great deal of potential and that he would be happy to recommend Victor for a tech lead position that was coming open in the next month or so if he was interested.

Victor was taken aback. The unexpected compliment and offer of support when applying to a job he thought he would have to wait at least another few years to qualify for surprised him, but also made him realize that he had been underestimating himself the whole time. He thanked his manager for his support and committed to applying for the new position once the posting became available.

Victor took some time to reflect on his work and began to see the tangible evidence of his progress—the successful projects he had completed, the positive feedback from his colleagues, and the respect he had earned from his superiors. In that moment of realization, he felt a weight lift off his shoulders. He realized that he had been too hard on himself, too blinded by his own self-criticism to see how far he had come. He was a perfectionist at heart and truly believed that until he had mastered EVERY skill at his current level, he wasn't ready to move up.

He now understands that while it is important to strive for excellence, it is equally important to acknowledge and celebrate his achievements along the way. Victor began preparing for the next step in his career. He reached out to three potential mentors and settled on one whom he thought was the right fit to encourage his progress. One of the habits he had been putting off was to join an industry networking association to meet people and learn about new opportunities. On the recommendation of his mentor, he joined one that meets in person monthly and holds quarterly workshops.

With a newfound sense of confidence and clarity, Victor decided to set new goals for himself, confident in his ability to achieve them. He learned the importance of accountability and self-awareness in habit-building, including how acknowledging progress can fuel motivation and drive success. He put a habit-tracking plan in place and now takes the time to assess and evaluate his progress on an ongoing basis. Victor made a conscious effort to acknowledge and celebrate his wins and to embrace the journey of growth and development.

Documenting changes and tracking progress is essential for success; otherwise, like Victor, it's easy to stagnate by keeping our focus too restricted to see our own progress or lack thereof. Seeing the big picture is necessary to keep moving forward. This chapter overviews how to keep track of your progress and exercise accountability to strengthen your willpower and resilience.

The Importance Of Tracking Results

It can be tempting to believe that you don't need to track your habits because the results will speak for themselves, but the truth is that you are more likely to be successful if you do. New habits are said to fail about 80% of the time on the first try, but tracking the habit can increase the chance of success. Participants in a weight loss program who recorded their attendance at meetings and food intake lost double the amount of weight of participants who did not.[1,2]

Tracking results is the seventh pillar of habit building and this provides four benefits:

1. <u>Organization and Planning</u>: It's impossible to know where you're headed without a plan. As the saying goes, a

goal without a plan is just a wish! You may eventually establish a habit or hit a goal, but without having your plan clearly laid out, you won't be nearly as productive as you could have been. This holds for goals that require little planning to implement and those that are more complex and must be carefully scheduled and monitored.

2. <u>Feedback</u>: Feedback helps us keep it real. It's hard to be dishonest when the numbers are staring you in the face! How often did you perform each habit last week? Last month? It's easy to overestimate how well we're doing when implementing something new, and we are often tempted to cut corners or even "cheat" on our plan. Feedback shows where you are doing well and where you can improve for the best results and forces us to own up to our successes and failures.

3. <u>Improve Efficiency</u>: Sometimes, the way we are doing something isn't the most efficient or effective, but it's hard to know if you aren't keeping track and analyzing your performance. By tracking processes and results, you can catch loopholes and inefficiencies in your processes, which allows you to implement better practices. Why not achieve the same or better results with the same amount of effort?

4. <u>Evidence and Motivation</u>: Seeing your accomplishments in black and white can help you believe in your strengths and capabilities. It's motivating to see just how far you've come when confronting a rough patch. Tracking can help you persevere through challenges and hardships on your journey.

Your Results Tracking Kit

A habit result tracking kit is more than just a simple habit tracker where you check off results. It's an all-in-one package that includes all the steps needed to plan, track, and assess your progress.

It consists of these basic elements:

1. <u>Planner</u>. It's great to make a list of all the habits you wish to make, but you need to consider how you are going to make them happen! You must plan for success. A good tracker includes a calendar for scheduling activities, a checklist or a notes area for listing the things you may need for each habit, and a spot for resources or contacts.

You can't check off a weekly therapy appointment if you don't choose a date, have the therapist's contact information, book it, note it on your calendar, and then show up. Good planning makes it easier to follow through and increases your chances of success.

2. <u>Recording/Tracking</u>. This is the part that most people think of when they hear "habit tracker," and mostly visualize a simple checklist. Checklists are great, and for some habits, they are enough. However, more is needed for other habits. Keeping a record of your progress can include a variety of different activities, including:

Journaling or Note-taking: Particularly when a habit is difficult or has delayed gratification, a journal of your thoughts, feelings, and observations can help improve your approach.

Bullet Journaling: This method has been shown to allow users the flexibility to combine meaningful elements such as mood and engage in reflective thinking. The flexible analog format can be a more personal approach for some people.[3]

Photos and Videos: Visual proof of how far you've come can keep you motivated. If your goal is to participate in an artistic activity 30 minutes a day, photos of your works in progress can be inspiring. Recordings of yourself speaking a new language or participating in physical activity can help you observe your development.

Collecting Feedback: When habits are based on performance, we can request feedback to see how we are doing. Someone who takes up a new sport can check their progress in a number of ways, including asking for feedback from a coach or trainer.

If your goal as a manager is to be a better mentor and more approachable to your team, asking for anonymous feedback or testimonials could help you adjust your approach. In general, medical test results, receipts, interviews, and written feedback are just some of the ways you can collect data on your progress on different habits.

3. <u>Checking and Analyzing</u>: Once you've collected all your data, it's time to analyze it. Are you going to create charts and graphs? How often will you analyze the data? Many people opt for a combination of weekly, monthly, quarterly, and annual. Based on the trends you identify,

you can see how well you have been able to form the new habits you desire.

Hopefully, you will see positive trends using this method. Sometimes, you might find that no matter how hard you try, certain habits just don't stick. What can you do?

Consider revising or adjusting the habit to be more attainable right now. If you plan to spend an hour a day outside but are struggling to make it happen, why not start with 15 minutes a day and work your way up? In tough cases, you may just have to swap the habit you want to achieve for something else temporarily until something changes. Major life changes, including accidents and illness, can make pursuing some habits impossible or impractical over the short or long term. Adapting your goals is essential to not get discouraged.

Habit Tracker Apps

These applications are particularly popular because they can take the guesswork out of keeping on track. The more ambitious ones can help with planning, tracking, and evaluating, saving you the time and effort of putting a tracker together yourself. Some of the more popular apps include:

1. *Coach.me*: This application is for those who want a more community feel when building habits. You join a community of people working on the same habit, track your goals, and receive advice from life coaches in the group. The basic app is free, but the paid version grants access to one-on-one coaching.

2. *Habitify*: A daily habit tracker that provides reminders, generates weekly and monthly reports, and has a built-in note function. The free app has limited functionality, such as a restricted number of habits you can track, but the paid version provides more functionality.

3. *Way of Life*: This app makes habits visible by color-coding positive and negative trends and shows progress in easy-to-read graphs. You can chart three habits for free or pay for the premium app to get access to more.[4,5]

Create a different goal. If the goal of maintaining a certain habit isn't working out for you, perhaps it would be a good idea to think about the possibility that you could switch to a different habit that helps you achieve the same goal.

Action Steps

1. *Create a habit-tracking kit of your own using the elements included in this chapter.*

Remember to account for habit planning and organization, tracking, and analyzing trends and results. If you prefer a tracker that is already put together, consider an app or a pre-made product you can purchase.

2. *Choose three habits to track over the next month.*

At the end of the month, evaluate the overall usefulness of the tracker and make any changes as necessary moving forward.

Habit tracking is the glue that holds everything together by making it clear and simple to follow your plan, providing feedback for your assessment, and allowing space for recalibrating your plans when needed. Still, despite our best efforts, sometimes we relapse and return to our old ways, re-adopting the bad habits we have worked so hard to break. Tracking is the last pillar of habit building but your journey doesn't end with just monitoring your progress. Chapter 9 provides you with resources and a plan to get back on track when relapse occurs.

Chapter Summary

- Tracking habits is an essential part of habit-building success.
- Habit tracking includes planning, tracking compliance, and assessing and evaluating results.
- Tracking provides feedback, motivation, and an unbiased picture of your progress and attainment.
- Tracking can also help you identify habits or goals that aren't working so you can realign them to your current situation and be more successful.

DETOUR OR DEAD END?

NAVIGATE THE ROADBLOCKS TO HABIT CONSISTENCY AND FIND YOUR WAY BACK AGAIN TO YOUR GOALS

Whitney is a passionate writer who has been diligently working on her first novel for months. She spent countless hours each day crafting her story, pouring her heart and soul into every word. Whitney was determined to see her dream of becoming a published author come true, but first, she needed to finish her book!

She set a daily writing goal of 500 words and met it faithfully for the first three months. Suddenly, her words dried up. Whitney went through a period of intense self-doubt and creative block. She struggled to find inspiration and motivation to continue working on her novel, and her daily writing goal turned into a weekly writing goal that was eventually abandoned altogether. Frustrated and overwhelmed, Whitney found herself procrastinating more and more, avoiding her writing desk and making excuses for why she couldn't work on her book.

Weeks turned into months, and Whitney's novel remained unfinished. She was frustrated with herself and embarrassed that she had ever thought she could call herself a writer. For the next six months, she didn't open the document that contained her draft at all.

It was a chance meeting at a friend's get-together with another aspiring author that gave Whitney a moment of clarity as she reflected on her stalled progress. Discussing writing with someone else helped her understand that she was not alone in struggling to maintain a consistent writing routine. Whitney hadn't realized that her isolation was making things worse since she had no one to share her ups and downs with. She realized that she had allowed her fear of failure and perfectionism to hold her back from pursuing her novel. Rather than embracing the challenges of the writing process, she let her doubts and insecurities dictate her actions.

Determined to break out of her creative rut, Whitney made a conscious decision to confront her fears and restart her writing habit. She contacted the author she met earlier and joined her writing group where she could share her work and receive feedback from others. She also committed to establishing a consistent writing routine, setting aside dedicated time each day to work on her novel.

Whitney joined an online writing challenge and updated her daily word count. The online challenge site provided an upward graph of each participant's writing progression, allowing her to visualize her progress and keeping her accountable. With each word she wrote, Whitney felt her confidence and inspiration returning, fueling her determination to see her novel through to the end.

Though Whitney didn't meet her 500-word-a-day goal every day, the data showed that she met her goal 87% of the time. First draft in hand, Whitney committed to continuing her writing habit and added an additional 30 minutes a day to edit her work. Whenever Whitney skipped more than three days of writing in a row and feared she was relapsing into her old habit of not writing at all, she went back to the progress chart, called her writing friend, or posted on a forum to get back on track.

Relapse, or returning to old habits, is expected when it comes to forging new habits. This chapter focuses on understanding how to learn from failure and resume routines after a relapse, as well as figuring out ways to prevent relapse in the future. This chapter also demystifies relapse, explaining its definition, causes, and consequences in detail.

It's important to understand that everyone relapses in some areas, and it's very common to have temptations that are too intense to resist. However, some relapses are more harmful than others, depending on each person's circumstances. Failing at something doesn't make you a failure or mean it's not worth trying again.

The information in this chapter is not meant to address the types of relapses that are dangerous to one's health, such as substance abuse. Please seek professional help if you are suffering the type of relapse you cannot handle alone.

Relapse Defined

The term "relapse" is most commonly used to describe a setback in terms of an illness or an addiction, a return to a worsened state.[1] However, it is appropriate to use it when referring to habits as well, as it signifies a return to harmful behavior patterns, particularly when under the influence of stress, trauma, or major life changes.

Relapse into old habits can occur when habit cues activate old behaviors, when prior routine cues activate the unwanted habit, or when memory cues are activated. Eliminating a behavior does not eliminate the memory connection to it. It's important to note that breaking bad habits is less about willpower than it is about breaking the cues that trigger the habit.[2]

Sliding back into bad habits can be discouraging and make us feel like we shouldn't even bother trying to change things, but it's important to put failure into perspective and realize that it is a natural part of habit formation. Most things in life are not permanent states of being. We are constantly striving for improvement, and habits are no exception.[3]

Would it be nice just to choose a new habit and stick to it? Of course! Unfortunately, the habits with the biggest long-term payoffs are often the ones that are the most difficult to stick to at first. The upside is that they are worth pursuing, even if it takes a few tries to make them stick.

In addiction services, relapse is seen as a gradual process, not an all-or-nothing event.[4] While we often applaud people for the all-or-nothing approach (for example, quitting smoking cold turkey), it's not really the only way to quit an addiction or a bad habit. Decreasing from a pack a day to one cigarette at lunch is changing the habit, even if it takes longer. Being cigarette-free for six months and sneaking one on a night out can turn into a full-blown relapse if you decide that it's an abject failure on your part to be a non-smoker.

Changing our mindset about how we view our relapses can make the difference between giving up for good or trying again. There are lessons to be learned from failure. By looking into what caused and contributed to a relapse, we can learn how to avoid them in the future. Anticipating and preparing for relapse triggers can give us a better chance of success.

If another relapse occurs, we will be better prepared to cope and recover quickly. We can find help and support, prevent major damage, and prepare resources to get back on track.

Common Causes Of Relapse

<u>Stress</u>: Stress can be the sneaky culprit behind a good habit's temporary disappearance. Earlier in the book, we

discussed how often bad habits are coping mechanisms or ways of avoiding unpleasant things. Avoidance, procrastination, and seeking comfort in the form of food, drink, or other unhealthy habits are common.

Boredom: Boredom can lead us to seek out activities or substances that bring us that hit of excitement or happiness, and often it's the most convenient option that catches our attention.

Complacency: When we take for granted that a habit is engrained too soon, we run the risk of dropping it without noticing. Tracking helps us not overestimate just how often we drink eight glasses of water daily rather than relying on memory.

Change in routine: Habits rely on routine, and they often become almost automatic. A change in routine can cause a change in what triggers the habit or can make the habit more difficult to maintain.

Temptations and Triggers: Good habits are often undertaken in an attempt to break free from temptations and triggers that can be like the siren call that you know you should ignore but can't help but listen to. Often, when we are confronted with them after a period without them, it is difficult not to give in "just this once."

The RAIN Model: A Mindfulness Self-Compassion Framework For Dealing With Relapse

The RAIN model is a four-step mindfulness self-compassion process that can help deal with relapse or any negative emotions or experiences that may affect habit formation and consistency. It was created by Tara Brach, a psychologist and meditation teacher, and it encompasses four key steps: 1) Recognize, 2) Allow, 3) Investigate, and 4) Nurture.[5]

1. <u>Recognize what is going on</u>. You cannot address a problem that you don't see. The old cliche of *admitting that you have a problem is the first step* is true. Ideally, you will be able to recognize the signs that you are sliding into old habits before you completely abandon new habits, but even recognizing it after the fact is a step in the right direction. This is where habit tracking can be a valuable tool. Your tracker will show you when a trend changes likely before you consciously realize it on your own. This can help you minimize the amount of backsliding that occurs before you take corrective action.

Recognition also applies to your feelings and behaviors at the moment. There is always a space between what you are feeling and how you choose to behave. Taking that second to acknowledge how you are feeling and what behavior it is making you want to do may be enough for you to make a different, better choice instead.

Being aware of your emotions is an important step in making sure that they do not control you. You may not be able to control the emotion that pops up in any given situation, but you can choose what to do with it once you recognize it. Give in? Or make a conscious choice to manage our reactions to it?

2. <u>Allow the experience to be just as it is</u>: This step is tough. Once you recognize what is happening, you instinctively jump in and fix it. To a certain extent, you can temporarily fix part of the problem by choosing a different behavior. However, the underlying trigger or emotion making you want to go back to your old habits will still be there. Thinking that you can continue to ignore that forever is a recipe for failure.

Giving yourself time to feel the emotion or recognize what has changed that is making you want to revert to old patterns is imperative. Deepen your attention to your emotions, thought patterns, sensations, and environment. Allow yourself the permission to really feel things. Avoiding or suppressing negative emotions is a surefire way to begin using negative coping mechanisms to block them out.

3. <u>Investigate</u>: Once you've sat in (probably uncomfortable!) silence with yourself, it's time to get to the bottom of what is going on beyond the obvious. It's easy to identify that you are feeling anxious. It's more difficult to pinpoint why, particularly if there isn't an obvious reason. You don't have to go through the Five W's, but it is an option if you're not sure where else to start. What are you feeling? Where does it manifest in the

body? Why is this happening? When do you notice it most? Who or what triggers these feelings?

Once you have asked yourself these questions, ask any others that may come to mind. This is not a one-time exercise, so be patient. You may need to come back to this again and again.

4. <u>Nurture with self-compassion</u>: By recognizing your suffering and giving yourself the self-compassion required to heal, you can begin to give yourself what you need. What would serve you best at this moment? Look beyond the knee-jerk reaction of your old, unhealthy comforts to what you need. It might be tempting to eat an entire box of donuts, but what your body might need is a nourishing bowl of soup.

The gestures of kindness might not even be physical actions but rather a reframing of negative thoughts and self-shame into more encouraging ones. Nurturing does not mean giving up and giving in to self-pity. Instead, it means having the courage to give yourself what it needs to heal so that you can try again. It's about self-love and self-empowerment in both a spiritual and very practical sense.[5]

Recovery From Relapse

We can often be our worst critics, giving ourselves a harder time than those around us. In order to recover from a habit relapse, you need to first be in the right mindset to move forward. Imagine a friend being in the same situation. What would you wish for them? Do the same for yourself.

1. Forgive yourself: Failing at something is hard. Relapsing, sometimes multiple times, is discouraging. Practice self-forgiveness. Be gentle with yourself at first, and then once you're ready, recommit to the work of trying again. You can forgive yourself the imperfection of being human AND be disciplined enough to know that you will recommit.

2. Learn from it: Every failure has something to teach you if you look at it as a lesson and an opportunity to come back stronger. Once the frustration and disappointment subside, look for the lesson and make the necessary changes to avoid the same fate next time.

3. Recommit: Work on reigniting the habit fire with renewed determination. You must go into it 100% committed, not anxiously worrying about failing again.

4. Celebrate progress: Every step counts, so celebrate even the smallest victories on the path to re-establishing your new habit.

Try Again

1. Start at the beginning: Go back to the beginning and remind yourself of your *why*. What will this habit bring to your life? Why is it worth the effort? Go through the steps in the previous chapters and reevaluate what you could do differently when you try again.

2. <u>Avoid triggers and distractions</u>: Particularly at the beginning, make an effort to avoid those people, places, or things that are triggers or distractions to the habit you are trying to build. Avoid places with negative associations and memories, rethink your social group, and take some time to focus inward.

3. <u>Get in some quick wins</u>: Consider getting back into the game with a small success. Think as small as 60 seconds! The idea is simply to feel a sense of success in the area in which you failed. If the goal was to eat a homemade meal each night and you spent the last two weeks eating take-out, start by eating something simple, like a sandwich that takes no more than a minute or two to make. If you've stopped exercising, run on the spot for a minute. Sounds silly, but it gets you back into the habit in a way that is almost guaranteed success.

4. <u>Manage your expectations</u>: Sometimes, we quit or fail at something because our expectations are too high to be realistic. This is where focusing on your systems over individual goals comes in handy. Failing to bring in your goal of $20,000 a year from your investments is focusing on goals.

The habit of investing for financial independence in retirement sees even half that amount as a step in the right direction. By tracking that habit, accessing the right resources, and staying consistent, you can work toward increasing that amount over time while not getting overwhelmed and discouraged over a specific dollar amount.

Action Steps

1. *RAIN Model.*

Think about the last time you reverted back to an old, unwanted habit that you have yet to recover from. Use the RAIN model of self-compassion to help deal with the relapse and put you in the right frame of mind to start over.

2. *Start Again.*

Once you are mentally ready, work through the "Try Again" steps to restart your desired habit. Start at the beginning, avoid triggers and distractions, get in some quick wins, and manage your expectations.

In previous chapters, we talked about the seven pillars of habit building. More than understanding the principles of habits, you need to arm yourself with pragmatics. You now have the tools you need to tackle setbacks and see them as part of the process, not the end of the road. In Chapter 10, we put everything together in a workbook-style format, where you can put the lessons in the book to even more use than you already have been.

Chapter Summary

- Habit relapse is when we return to old, unwanted, or harmful habits after a period of leaving them behind.

- The RAIN method of self-compassion can help work through the feelings of anger, disappointment, and frustration of failing at a habit, and provides a framework for understanding what happened.
- Recovery includes forgiving yourself, learning from the failure, recommitting to the habit, and preparing to celebrate small successes.
- Try Again! Start at the beginning, avoid triggers and distractions, get in some quick wins, and manage your expectations.

DON'T STRESS OVER PERFECTION

YOUR WORKBOOK TO NURTURING HABITS THAT
WITHSTAND TIME TO SUPPORT YOUR JOURNEY
TO LASTING CHANGE

T his chapter is your chance to put everything you've learned in this book to use. It contains a summary of each chapter, followed by resources and activities designed to help you successfully put the lessons into practice. If you haven't completed any of the action steps at the end of each chapter, this is the place to start! If you have been completing the action steps along the way, this chapter is a chance to dig deeper and make even more progress.

Chapter 1

We started the book with a breakdown of the most basic habit formation formula:

Cue >Behavior >Reward

The *cue* is something that triggers the behavior or the

habit. The *behavior* is the habit. Finally, the *reward* is what the habit gives you that makes it addictive.[1]

Bad habits are often easier and more addictive because they provide immediate gratification that makes us feel good, even if it's bad for us in the long run. Bad habits are often **coping** *mechanisms* we use to avoid the negative emotions that stem from certain triggers, like avoiding feeling stress or anxiety.

Good habits can be more difficult to sustain because the cues are often not as obvious, and the payoff often isn't in the form of instant gratification. You won't lose 10 pounds after eating one salad, nor will your muscles pop after one weight-training session.

Identifying our cues, habits, and coping mechanisms is key to becoming more self-aware and bringing those automatic bad habits into the light. Choosing which good habits we want to cultivate sets us up for the rest of the activities in the workbook.

Activities

1. Why do bad habits make us feel so good? List 3-5 bad habits that make you feel good in the moment, even though you know they are bad for you in the long run. What are the cues for each behavior?

2. What good habits could you replace them with? What cues could you implement to help make the habits stick?

3. What are your coping mechanisms for stressful, upsetting, or otherwise negative situations? Make two lists:

One for positive coping mechanisms and another for negative ones.

Positive	Negative

Coping Mechanisms

4. What could you replace your negative coping mechanisms with? Would any of your positive ones work, or do you need to replace them with something completely new? Reflect on your negative coping mechanisms. Can you identify WHY you do them?

5. Which habits are you holding onto from childhood that no longer serve you? What could you replace them with instead?

<u>Chapter 2</u>

This chapter encourages you to become more **self**-*aware*, both *internally*, as in how you see yourself, and *externally*, becoming aware of how others see you. We learned how to conduct an analysis of personal Strengths, Weaknesses, Opportunities, and Threats (SWOT).[2]

You were encouraged to apply that information to a *personal growth plan*, focusing on the five areas of personal growth: Physical, Mental, Emotional, Social, and Spiritual.

The *Eisenhower Matrix* helped categorize your priorities based on what is:

1- Urgent, Important, *2-* Not Urgent, Important, *3-* Urgent, Not Important, *4-* Not Urgent, Not Important.[3]

Thinking about your daily schedule, which activities are taking up unnecessary time that could be better used in the pursuit of better habits?

Then you were introduced to *SMART Goals* (Specific, Measurable, Achievable, Relevant, and Timebound) to narrow down the specific areas of focus, highlighting the habits that you would need to cultivate to achieve them.[4]

Activities

1. Conduct a personal SWOT Analysis.

PERSONAL SWOT ANALYSIS

Strengths	Weaknesses	Opportunities	Threats

2. Identify at least one thing you would like to work on in each of the five areas of personal growth.

- Physical:
- Mental:
- Emotional:
- Social:
- Spiritual:

3. Create your own *Eisenhower Matrix*, prioritizing the activities of a typical day. Which unimportant activities can you delegate, minimize, or drop? Which important but not urgent activities should you be spending more time on?

4. Choose an area of improvement and create a SMART goal that will create the habit of tracking progress and

reaching milestones.

- Specific:
- Measurable:
- Achievable:
- Relevant:
- Timebound:

Chapter 3

We delved into some uncomfortable territory, identifying the negative triggers that lead to some bad habits. A *trigger* is an environmental factor, such as a person, place, thing, or time, that elicits an emotion. *Negative triggers* can often make us want to turn to coping mechanisms to manage how they make us feel.

In identifying our triggers, recognizing what is happening in our bodies at the time can help change behavior. The first step to change is recognizing the trigger and how it typically makes you think, feel, and behave. The *BEST model* can help identify:

- *B:* The Behavior you want to do as a result of the trigger
- *E:* The Emotions you are feeling
- *S:* The sensations in your body, such as the fight or flight response
- *T:* The thoughts that are sparked by the trigger[5]

To change a bad habit, we must be able to do three things:

Have a moment of awareness: We can't change what we don't recognize.

Resist urges: We must resist the urge to react the same way again and make space for a better alternative.

Have a replacement behavior: If you aren't going to do what you've always done, what then?

Activities

1. Which two bad habits would you most like to break? Identify the triggers for each habit.

2. Choose one of the habits above. Work through the BEST model for it.

B	Behavior
E	Emotions
S	Sensations
T	Thoughts

3. How can you prepare to have a moment of awareness, resist the urge, and have a replacement behavior prepared for this bad habit?

Chapter 4

We started moving on from *negative triggers* to implementing *positive triggers* to encourage the growth of good habits. We took the *ABC Model* and went even further by including the updated *ABCDE Model.*

The classic model is:

- *A:* Antecedent
- *B:* Behavior
- *C:* Consequence.

The expanded model includes:

- *D:* Disputing an irrational belief
- *E:* Resulting in a new effect[6]

We learned how *habit stacking* and *habit pairing* can be implemented in conjunction with this model to replace negative triggers with more positive ones and also to make new habits easier to stick to.

Finally, we ended the chapter by learning about the importance of *rewards.* Not just any rewards, but choosing specific rewards that are best suited to you. Rewards can be *intrinsic or extrinsic,* and the right one depends on the habit you are trying to cultivate and your personal preferences.

Activities

1. Create your own ABC(DE) Model. This model works best for targeting one specific behavior change at a time. Name one bad habit you would like to change and focus on one specific behavior using the ABC(DE) Model as your guide.

Behavior:

- A:
- B:
- C:
- D:
- E:

2. Stack or Pair. Which behaviors could you stack or pair with a new habit you would like to cultivate?

3. Choose your rewards. Make a list of intrinsic and extrinsic rewards you feel could be implemented when cultivating new, good habits. Keep this list handy so that it's easy to celebrate when the time comes.

Chapter 5

In Chapter 5, we learned that our *environment* can set the tone for a particular mindset, trigger associations, and feature specific negative triggers that affect our habits.

The world around us influences our *behavior, mood, and cognition*. Sometimes, our environment is the biggest factor influencing our habits. We also learned that *optimizing our environment* can make it easier to engage in healthy habits.

Removing Distractions can help improve focus when working or allow for deeper relaxation when trying to sleep. *Adding Positive Cues* can remind or inspire you to think about initiating a good habit. *Creating Specific Zones* helps prompt you to perform specific activities.

When we aren't in control of our environment, we can try to improve it through *communication* with those who share it, *setting boundaries* where possible, *negotiation* and compromise, and *adapting* to our surroundings. Sometimes, we need to consider a *change of location* altogether.

Activities

1. Assess your environment: Identify areas of your environment that may be triggering negative behaviors or hindering your ability to engage in healthy habits.

2. Create specific zones: Establish specific zones within your environment to prompt and facilitate particular activities-focused productivity.

3. Remove distractions: Identify and eliminate distractions in your environment that may be impeding your focus or productivity.

4. Consider a change of location: If your current environment consistently hinders your ability to engage in

healthy habits despite efforts to optimize it, consider exploring a change of location.

Chapter 6

At the beginning of the book, the formula for habit formation was presented as *Cue > Behavior > Reward*. In Chapter 6, we added another dimension to the *habit loop*:

$$Cue > Craving > Response\ (Behavior) > Reward$$

Craving, the added element, is our desire to engage in the behavior that creates the habit. Cravings can make a habit more appealing to do. Other ways to make a new habit more appealing to stick with involves making it *Obvious, Attractive, Easy, or Satisfying*.[7]

Focusing on systems rather than goals is better for long-term habit formation. Goals play a role in the motivational aspect of habit maintenance, but ideally, habits should be lifelong, or at least long-term. Short-term goals are more like stepping stones.

Instead, build habits around one or more of the ten most common areas of improvement: *Time, Sleep, Food, Fitness, Space, Play, People, Money, Spirit, or Voice*.[8] And remember, flexibility and adaptability are key, as life changes in unexpected ways.

Activities

1. Optimize habit appeal: Make your habits more appealing and sustainable by focusing on making them Obvious, Attractive, Easy, or Satisfying. Choose one or two habits you are having a particularly hard time being consistent about and optimize them.

2. Build habits around key areas of improvement: Direct your habit-building efforts toward one or more of the ten most common areas of improvement: Time, Sleep, Food, Fitness, Space, Play, People, Money, Spirit, or Voice. Choose habits that align with your values and priorities in these areas, focusing on sustainable behaviors that contribute to overall well-being and fulfillment.

3. Develop problem-solving skills to improve flexibility and adaptability: Break down problems into manageable steps, brainstorm potential solutions, and experiment with different approaches.

Chapter 7

When we are trying to change something, doing it alone is not always the most effective course of action. It can be hard to keep ourselves accountable, leading to discouragement. It can be isolating and overwhelming. Finding a *support system* can make a world of difference.

Support systems provide *accountability*. They can serve as sources of *motivation, discipline, and positive reinforcement*. Professional support systems can offer *teaching, coaching, and advice*. And finding others who have *shared interests* can make the habit a part of a shared social experience, making it more fun and less work. Depending on your needs, support systems can be informal, semi-formal, or formal/professional in nature, or a mix of all three.

They can be family, friends, mentors, coaches, or community members who encourage personal growth and provide support to help you be successful.

Along with support systems, Chapter 7 discussed the importance of finding the right *resources* to support your journey. Books, podcasts, and vision boards can all be useful. Below is a checklist of resources, with additional space to add your ideas.

RESOURCES TO SUPPORT YOUR HABIT JOURNEY

☐ BOOKS

☐ WEBSITES

☐ PODCASTS

☐ COURSES

☐ VISION BOARDS

☐ VIDEOS

☐ *ADD YOUR OWN IDEAS BELOW*

☐

☐

☐

☐

☐

☐

☐

☐

Activities

1. Check out the resources listed above. Complete the list with specific resources that are appropriate for one of your habits. Make separate lists for different types of habits.

2. Seek out like-minded individuals: Look for others who share your goals or interests and could provide valuable support and companionship along your journey. Join online communities, attend local meetups or workshops, or reach out to friends or acquaintances who may be on a similar path.

3. Join a structured program: Consider participating in a structured program or workshop designed to support individuals in making positive changes in their lives. Even a short-term program can make pursuing a new habit feel more formal.

4. Engage in reciprocal support: Offer support to others in your network who are also working towards their goals. By giving back and providing encouragement to others, you can strengthen your commitment and motivation while building deeper connections within your support system.

Chapter 8

Chapter 8 is all about the why and how of habit tracking. *Habit tracking* is the glue that holds everything together by making it *clear and simple* to follow your plan, *providing feedback* for your assessment, and allowing space for *recalibrating your plans* when needed.

A *habit tracking kit* can be bought or made, and can be a physical kit or an online one, like one of the many habit tracker apps available. A good habit tracker should include room for the *planning* stage, an actual tracker or *checklist*, space for a *journal or notes, photos, videos, and feedback*. It should also provide the data to adequately check and analyze progress.

Activities

1. Use the following habit tracker or look for something similar to check off your daily progress over the next month.

HABIT TRACKER   MONTH:

2. Next, take the time to investigate and choose the overall system that will work for you. It might be a paper-based option, an online website, or a habit tracker app. Continue to use the checklist above to get started while you put your long-term plan into place.

Chapter 9

Even the best-laid plans can go wrong, and Chapter 9 provides the resources you need to get back on track. The term *"relapse"* is most commonly used to describe a setback in terms of an illness or an addiction, a return to a worsened state. However, it is appropriate to use when referring to habits as well, as it signifies *a return to harmful behavior patterns*, particularly when under the influence of stress, trauma, or major life changes. This often occurs when we experience stress, boredom, complacency, a change in routine, or give in to temptations or triggers.[9]

When this happens, it's easy to get caught in a cycle of frustration, self-doubt, and discouragement. The *RAIN model* is a four-step *mindfulness self-compassion process* that can help deal with relapse or any negative emotions or experiences that may affect habit formation and consistency. It was created by Tara Brach, a psychologist and meditation teacher, and it encompasses four key steps: *1) Recognize, 2) Allow, 3) Investigate, and 4) Nurture.*[10]

Work through the steps to recover from failure by forgiving yourself for not succeeding, learning from the failure, recommitting to trying again, and celebrating your progress. When you're ready to try again, rediscover your reason why before beginning. Avoid triggers and distractions, get in some quick wins with micro-habits, and manage your expectations. Sometimes, it takes multiple attempts before seeing success.

Activities

1. Recognize the relapse: Acknowledge and accept that you have experienced a setback in your habit formation journey. Avoid denial or minimizing the relapse and instead confront it head-on with honesty and self-awareness. Permit yourself to experience the emotions that arise from the relapse, whether it's frustration, disappointment, or self-doubt.

2. Learn from the failure: Extract valuable lessons from the relapse by identifying what went wrong and why. Use this information to adjust your approach, address any underlying issues, and develop strategies to prevent future relapses.

3. Rediscover your reason why: Take time to reconnect with your underlying motivation and purpose for pursuing the habit in the first place.

CONCLUSION

More than a book that simply talks about habits, this has been about putting that information into action. Think back to the reason you chose to read this book in the first place. Were you frustrated at not being able to break a particularly bad habit? Or was there a new habit you have been having difficulty getting to stick?

Now that you've made it to the end of the last chapter, how has your outlook on habits changed? Have you taken the time to put the action items in place? Or are you exactly where you were at the start, doing the same things and getting the same results? If you haven't made the time to implement the action items, why not?

It's time to apply what you've learned to change your life for the better by leaving behind the habits that no longer serve you and building the ones that do. Cultivate habits that work for you, rather than against you. Understand that building a support system and accessing the right resources at the right time are essential for ongoing success. And prepare for the possibility of setbacks and even failure from time to time.

Is it the fear of failure that has stopped you from getting started? Remember that everything, including habits, is a journey. Most journeys aren't linear, but to make any progress, you must take the first step. Take some time to recognize that just by reading this book, you have already embarked on your journey. There's no turning back now!

It takes a lot of courage, determination, and commitment to choose to leave behind habits that are easy and feel good at the moment to pursue ones that are often harder to implement and don't provide instant gratification but that are ultimately better for you and the person you want to be. You may have to change your environment, the people you spend time with, your daily routines, and the instant gratification you get from those habits that you know are bad but feel oh-so-good!

As you read through the stories at the beginning of each chapter, could you relate to their dilemmas? Often, we can see what others need to do to change for the better before we can see what needs to be done in our own lives. By providing relatable examples, I hoped to provide the opportunity for you to reflect on your own habits and see that there are actionable steps you can take to make the changes you desire.

Only you can choose to keep moving forward on your self-improvement journey, but remember that you're not alone. You can return to these pages whenever you need to find inspiration, action items, and encouragement to keep going. Work through the action items at the end of the chapters and take your time completing the activities in the workbook in Chapter 10.

This is a marathon, not a sprint. Take the time you need to work through the challenges. You're aiming for long-term change, not short-term satisfaction. And you're already off to a great start.

OVER 10,000 PEOPLE HAVE ALREADY SUBSCRIBED. DID YOU TAKE YOUR CHANCE YET?

In general, around 50% of the people who start reading do not finish a book. You are the exception, and we are happy you took the time.

To honor this, we invite you to join our exclusive Thinknetic newsletter. You cannot find this subscription link anywhere else on the web but in our books!

Upon signing up, you'll receive two of our most popular bestselling books, highly acclaimed by readers like yourself. We sell copies of these books daily, but you will receive them as a gift. Additionally, you'll gain access to two transformative short sheets and enjoy complimentary access to all our upcoming e-books, completely free of charge!

This offer and our newsletter are free; you can unsubscribe anytime.

Here's everything you get:

✓ Critical Thinking For Complex Issues eBook   **($9.99 Value)**
✓ The Intelligent Reader's Guide To Reading eBook **($9.99 Value)**
✓ Break Your Thinking Patterns Sheet   **($4.99 Value)**
✓ Flex Your Wisdom Muscle Sheet   **($4.99 Value)**
✓ All our upcoming eBooks   **($199.80* Value)**

Total Value: $229.76

Go to thinknetic.net for the offer!

(Or simply scan the code with your camera)

SCAN ME

*If you download 20 of our books for free, this would equal a value of 199.80$

THE PEOPLE BEHIND THINKNETIC

Christoph Maurer, Founder and CEO

Christoph has always been a voracious reader with a writing talent. A bit less common, he has also been fascinated by business since he was a child. Consequently, after earning his degree in business management, he chose publishing as a full-time career. With his good friend of over 15 years, Michael, he founded Thinknetic. The company aims to build the most reader-centric original publishing house possible and become a household brand trusted by its dear readers. Practicing what he preaches, Christoph spends a considerable amount of time reading every day, deeply influenced by the examples set by Charlie Munger and Warren Buffet.

Michael Meisner, Founder and CEO

When Michael ventured into publishing books on Amazon, he discovered that his favorite topics—the intricacies of the human mind and behavior—were often tackled in a way that's too complex and unengaging. Thus, he dedicated himself to making his ideal a reality: books that effortlessly inform, entertain, and resonate with readers' everyday experiences, enabling them to enact enduring positive changes in their lives. Together with like-minded people, this ideal became his passion and profession. Michael is primarily in charge of steering the operational side of Thinknetic, as he continues to improve and extend the business.

Claire M. Umali, Publishing Manager

Collaborative work lies at the heart of crafting books, and keeping everyone on the same page is an essential task. Claire oversees all the stages of this collaboration, from researching to outlining and from writing to editing. In her free time, she writes online reviews and likes to bother her cats.

Farley Bermeo, Publishing Manager

Farley has a knack for storytelling and writing personal narratives, both mundane and the extraordinary. Combining his background in writing and experience in program management, he ensures that ideas are transformed into pages. He believes that a good story is better told with a cup of coffee.

Kathleen Sperduti, Writer

Kathleen Sperduti is an experienced teacher, writer, and editor with a graduate degree in Education. Kathleen runs a parent association for families of children with disabilities, complex medical diagnoses, and learning needs. Her portfolio includes blog posts, magazine articles, e-books, and academic articles on a variety of topics. In her spare time, she enjoys language learning, traveling, reading, and knitting.

Andrew Speno, Content Editor

Andrew is a teacher, writer, and editor. He has published two historical nonfiction books for middle-grade readers, a biography of Eddie Rickenbacker and the story of the 1928 Bunion Derby ultra-marathon. He enjoys cooking, attending live theater, and playing the ancient game of go.

Sandra Agarrat, Language Editor

Sandra Wall Agarrat is an experienced freelance academic editor/proofreader, writer, and researcher. Sandra holds graduate degrees in Public Policy and International Relations. Her portfolio of projects includes books, dissertations, theses, scholarly articles, and grant proposals.

Renell Bernardino, Layout Designer

Renell is our versatile publishing assistant and go-to graphic artist. His journey to becoming a graphic designer was a unique one. As an engineer who is passionate about hard sciences, his creative side often felt stifled in such a technical field. Seeking an outlet to exercise his artistic talents, Renell began exploring graphic design independently, mastering the craft through autodidactic avenues rather than formal classes or traditional education. His organic approach to learning allowed him to develop a style that is both innovative and deeply personal.

Jemarie Gumban, Hiring Manager

Jemarie is in charge of thoroughly examining and evaluating the profiles and potential of the many aspiring writers for Thinknetic. With an academic background in Applied Linguistics and a meaningful experience as an industrial worker, she approaches her work with a discerning eye and fresh outlook. Guided by her unique perspective, Jemarie derives fulfillment from turning a writer's desire to create motivational literature into tangible reality.

Evangeline Obiedo, Publishing Assistant

Evangeline diligently supports our books' journey, from the writing stage to connecting with our readers. Her commitment to detail permeates her work, encompassing tasks such as initiating profile evaluations and ensuring seamless delivery of our newsletters. Her love for learning extends into the real world— she loves traveling and experiencing new places and cultures.

REFERENCES

1. The Beauty of Bad Habits

1. Schaffner, A. K. (2023). 10 Most unhealthy coping mechanisms: A list. Positive Psychology. https://positivepsychology.com/unhealthy-coping-mechanisms/
2. Manson, M. (n.d.). Creating healthy habits: A practical guide. Mark Manson. https://markmanson.net/habits
3. Center for Responsive Schools. (n.d.). Making and breaking habits. https://www.crslearn.org/publication/building-sel-skills/making-breaking-habits/#:~:text=There%20will%20be%20times%20when,be%20changed%20at%20any%20age.
4. Byrne, K. A., Six, Stephanie G., Willis, Hunter C. (2021). Examining the effect of depressive symptoms on habit formation and habit-breaking. Journal of Behavior Therapy and Experimental Psychiatry, Volume 73:101676, https://doi.org/10.1016/j.jbtep.2021.101676.
5. Rutledge, T. (2021). Why bad habits are easy and good habits are hard. Psychology Today. https://www.psychologytoday.com/us/blog/the-healthy-journey/202108/why-bad-habits-are-easy-and-good-habits-are-hard

2. Pillar 1 - Say Goodbye To Your Old Self

1. Eurich, T. (2018). *What self-awareness really is (and how to cultivate it)*. Harvard Business Review. https://hbr.org/2018/01/what-self-awareness-really-is-and-how-to-cultivate-it
2. Puyt, R. W., Lie, F. B., & Wilderom, C. P. M. (2023). The origins of SWOT analysis. *Long Range Planning, 56*(3), 102304. https://doi.org/10.1016/j.lrp.2023.102304
3. Gomer, J., & Hill, J. (2015). *An essential guide to SWOT analysis*. Form Swift. http://mci.ei.columbia.edu/files/2012/12/An-Essential-Guide-to-SWOT-Analysis.pdf
4. Dyer, K. (2023). Daily healthy habits to reduce stress and increase longevity. *Journal of Interprofessional Education & Practice. Volume 30: 100593*. https://doi.org/10.1016/j.xjep.2022.100593.

5. Indeed Editorial Team. (Updated 2023, February 3). *5 Areas of personal growth (Plus tips for development).* Indeed. https://www.indeed.com/career-advice/career-development/areas-of-personal-growth

6. Kennedy, D. R., & Porter, A. L. (2022). The Illusion of Urgency. *American journal of pharmaceutical education, 86*(7), 8914. https://doi.org/10.5688/ajpe8914

7. Covey, S. (2020). *The 7 habits of highly effective people: 30th anniversary edition.* Simon & Schuster.

8. Team Asana. (2022). *The Eisenhower Matrix: How to prioritize your to-do list.* Asana. https://asana.com/resources/eisenhower-matrix

9. Herrity, J. (2023). *Guide on how to write SMART goals (with examples).* Indeed. https://www.indeed.com/career-advice/career-development/how-to-write-smart-goals

3. Pillar 2 - Who's Calling The Shots?

1. Hall, K. (2018). *Understanding the thoughts-feelings-behaviors connection.* https://www.ktherapy.ca/blog/2018/12/19/thoughts-and-reactions

2. Outlook Associates. (2019). *Handout 4: Triggers, cues, and high-risk situations.* https://outlookassociates.com/wp-content/uploads/2019/06/handout-triggers-cues.pdf

3. Bregman, P. (2015). *Quash your bad habits by knowing what triggers them.* Harvard Business Review. https://hbr.org/2015/10/quash-your-bad-habits-by-knowing-what-triggers-ociatesthem

4. Solis-Moreira, J. (2024). *How long does it really take to form a habit.* Scientific American. https://www.scientificamerican.com/article/how-long-does-it-really-take-to-form-a-habit/

4. Pillar 3 - The ABCs Of Habit Mastery

1. Field, T. A., Beeson, E. T., & Jones, L. K. (2015). The new ABCs: A practitioner's guide to neuroscience-informed cognitive-behavior therapy. *Journal of Mental Health Counseling, 37*(3), 206–220. https://doi.org/10.17744/1040-2861-37.3.206

2. Selva, J. (2018). *What is Albert Ellis's ABC model in CBT theory (Incl. pdf).* Positive Psychology. https://positivepsychology.com/albert-ellis-abc-model-rebt-cbt/

3. Seaver, M. (Updated 2023, March 31). *Habit stacking is the easiest way to make new habits last-here's how it works.* Real Simple. https://www.re-

alsimple.com/work-life/life-strategies/inspiration-motivation/habit-stacking

4. McKloskey, K., Johnson, B. (2019). Habits, quick and easy: Perceived complexity moderates the associations of contextual stability and rewards with behavioral automaticity. *Frontiers in Psychology 10:2019*. https://doi.org/10.3389/fpsyg.2019.01556

5. Mindful Self-Discipline. *Extrinsic Rewards.* https://www.mindful-selfdiscipline.com/extrinsic-rewards/

6. Verplanken, B., Orbell, S. (2022). Attitudes, habits, and behavior change. *Annual Review of Psychology 73:327-352.* https://doi.org/10.1146/annurev-psych-020821-011744

5. Pillar 4 - The Habitat of Good Habits

1. Lally, P., & Gardner, B. (2013). Promoting habit formation. *Health Psychology Review, 7(*sup1), S137–S158. https://doi.org/10.1080/17437199.2011.603640

2. Newport Institute. (2021). *How does your physical environment affect you and your mental health?* https://www.newportinstitute.com/resources/mental-health/physical-environment-affect-you/

3. Clear, J. (2018). *Atomic habits: Tiny habits, remarkable results.* New York: Avery. https://jamesclear.com/atomic-habits

4. Chu, M. (2017). *Why your environment is the biggest factor in changing your life. Willpower alone is not enough.* Inc. https://www.inc.com/melissa-chu/its-possible-to-design-your-environment-to-help-yo.html

5. Gardner, B., & Rebar, A. L. (2019). Habit formation and behavior change. In *Oxford research encyclopedia of psychology.* https://doi.org/10.1093/acrefore/9780190236557.013.129

6. Pillar 5 - Sticking Like Honey

1. Clear, J. (2018). *Atomic habits: Tiny habits, remarkable results.* New York: Avery. https://jamesclear.com/atomic-habits

2. Bregman, P. (2015). *Quash your bad habits by knowing what triggers them.* Harvard Business Review. https://hbr.org/2015/10/quash-your-bad-habits-by-knowing-what-triggers-ociatesthem

3. Coomer, S.H. (2020). *The Habit Trip.* Running Press. https://www.sarahhayscoomer.com/the-habit-trip

4. Gardner, B., & Rebar, A. L. (2019). Habit formation and behavior change. In *Oxford research encyclopedia of psychology.* https://doi.org/10.1093/acrefore/9780190236557.013.129

5. NIH. (Updated March 24, 2022). *What are sleep deprivation and deficiency?* National Heart, Lung, and Blood Institute (NIH). https://www.nhlbi.nih.gov/health/sleep-deprivation

6. van Timmeren, T., & de Wit, S. (2023). Instant habits versus flexible tenacity: Do implementation intentions accelerate habit formation? *Quarterly journal of experimental psychology (2006)*, *76*(11), 2479–2492. https://doi.org/10.1177/17470218221147024

7. Crockett, M. J., Braams, B. R., Clark, L., Tobler, P. N., Robbins, T. W., & Kalenscher, T. (2013). Restricting temptations: neural mechanisms of precommitment. *Neuron*, *79*(2), 391–401. https://doi.org/10.1016/j.neuron.2013.05.028

8. Oxford Learner's Dictionaries. (n.d.). *Flexibility.* https://www.ox-fordlearnersdictionaries.com/definition/english/flexibility

9. Oxford Learner's Dictionaries. (n.d.). *Adaptability.* https://www.oxfordlearnersdictionaries.com/definition/english/adaptability

7. Pillar 6 - Not Alone

1. Ufholz, K. (2020). Peer Support Groups for Weight Loss. *Current Cardiovasc Risk Rep* 14 (19)/ https://doi.org/10.1007/s12170-020-00654-4

2. Kwasnicka, D., Dombrowski, S. U., White, M., & Sniehotta, F. (2016). Theoretical explanations for maintenance of behaviour change: a systematic review of behaviour theories. *Health psychology review*, *10*(3), 277-296. https://doi.org/10.1080/17437199.2016.1151372

3. Haffner, S. (n.d.). *Are your friends' habits your habits?* https://www.stevehaffner.com/post/social-proximity-effect

4. Stan, D. L., Cutshall, S. M., Adams, T. F., Ghosh, K., Clark, M. M., Wieneke, K. C., Kebede, E. B., Donelan Dunlap, B. J., Ruddy, K. J., Hazelton, J. K., Butts, A. M., Jenkins, S. M., Croghan, I. T., & Bauer, B. A. (2020). Wellness Coaching: An Intervention to Increase Healthy Behavior in Breast Cancer Survivors. *Clinical journal of oncology nursing*, *24*(3), 305–315. https://doi.org/10.1188/20.CJON.305-315

5. Paudyal, n. (2018). *25 Websites other than social media to upgrade your life.* LifeHack. https://www.lifehack.org/318009/25-websites-other-than-social-media-upgrade-your-life

8. Pillar 7 - The Habit-Tracking Kit

1. Checkable Health. (2023). *The importance of tracking habits.* https://www.checkable.com/blogs/blog/the-importance-of-tracking-habits
2. Science Daily. (2008). *Keeping a food diary doubles weight loss, study suggests.* Kaiser Permanente. https://www.sciencedaily.com/releases/2008/07/080708080738.htm
3. Ayobi, A., Sonne, T., Marshall, P., & Cox, A. L. (2018). Flexible and Mindful Self-Tracking: Design Implications from Paper Bullet Journals. In *CHI 2018 - Proceedings of the 2018 CHI Conference on Human Factors in Computing Systems* (pp. 1-14). Article 28 Association for Computing Machinery (ACM). https://doi.org/10.1145/3173574.3173602
4. Parker, Haillie. (2023). *The 10 best habit tracker apps in 2024 (features, pricing).* Click Up. The 10 Best Habit Tracker Apps in 2024 (Features, Pricing) | ClickUp
5. Perry, E. (2023). *The 11 best habit tracker apps to build new behaviors.* Better Up. https://www.betterup.com/blog/best-habit-tracker-apps

9. Detour Or Dead End?

1. Merriam-Webster. (n.d.). *Relapse.* https://www.merriam-webster.com/dictionary/relapse
2. Wood, W., & Rünger, D. (2016). Psychology of habit. *Annual review of psychology, 67,* 289-314. https://doi.org/10.1146/annurev-psych-020821-011744
3. Thompson, C. (2015). *The art of relapse: How to stop falling back into old habits.* Experience Life by Time Life. https://experiencelife.lifetime.life/article/the-art-of-the-relapse/
4. Melemis, S. M. (2015). Focus: addiction: relapse prevention and the five rules of recovery. *The Yale journal of biology and medicine, 88*(3), 325. PMID: 26339217. https://www.ncbi.nlm.nih.gov/pmc/articles/PMC4553654/
5. Brach, T. (2020). *Blog-RAIN: A practice of radical compassion.* Tara Brach. https://www.tarabrach.com/rain-practice-radical-compassion/

10. Don't Stress Over Perfection

1. Manson, M. (n.d.). *Creating healthy habits: A practical guide.* Mark Manson. https://markmanson.net/habits

2. Gomer, J., & Hill, J. (2015). *An essential guide to SWOT analysis.* Form Swift. http://mci.ei.columbia.edu/files/2012/12/An-Essential-Guide-to-SWOT-Analysis.pdf

3. Team Asana. (2022). *The Eisenhower Matrix: How to prioritize your to-do list.* Asana. https://asana.com/resources/eisenhower-matrix

4. Herrity, J. (2023). *Guide on how to write SMART goals (with examples).* Indeed. https://www.indeed.com/career-advice/career-development/how-to-write-smart-goals

5. Outlook Associates. (2019). *Handout 4: Triggers, cues, and high-risk situations.* https://outlookassociates.com/wp-content/uploads/2019/06/handout-triggers-cues.pdf

6. Selva, J. (2018). *What is Albert Ellis's ABC model in CBT theory (Incl. pdf).* Positive Psychology. https://positivepsychology.com/albert-ellis-abc-model-rebt-cbt/

7. Clear, J. (2018). *Atomic habits: Tiny habits, remarkable results.* New York: Avery. https://jamesclear.com/atomic-habits

8. Coomer, S.H. (2020). *The Habit Trip.* Running Press. https://www.sarahhayscoomer.com/the-habit-trip

9. Merriam-Webster. (n.d.). *Relapse.* https://www.merriam-webster.com/dictionary/relapse

10. Brach, T. (2020). *Blog-RAIN: A practice of radical compassion.* Tara Brach. https://www.tarabrach.com/rain-practice-radical-compassion/

DISCLAIMER

The information contained in this book and its components, is meant to serve as a comprehensive collection of strategies that the author of this book has done research about. Summaries, strategies, tips and tricks are only recommendations by the author, and reading this book will not guarantee that one's results will exactly mirror the author's results.

The author of this book has made all reasonable efforts to provide current and accurate information for the readers of this book. The author and their associates will not be held liable for any unintentional errors or omissions that may be found, and for damages arising from the use or misuse of the information presented in this book.

Readers should exercise their own judgment and discretion in interpreting and applying the information to their specific circumstances. This book is not intended to replace professional advice (especially medical advice, diagnosis, or treatment). Readers are encouraged to seek appropriate professional guidance for their individual needs.

The material in the book may include information by third parties. Third party materials comprise of opinions expressed by their owners. As such, the author of this book does not assume responsibility or liability for any third party material or opinions.

The publication of third party material does not constitute the author's guarantee of any information, products, services, or opinions contained within third party material. Use of third party material does not guarantee that your results will mirror our results. Publication of such third party material is simply a recommendation and expression of the author's own opinion of that material.

Whether because of the progression of the Internet, or the unforeseen changes in company policy and editorial submission guidelines, what is stated as fact at the time of this writing may become outdated or inapplicable later.

Thinknetic is committed to respecting copyright laws and intellectual property rights. We have taken reasonable measures to ensure that all quotes, diagrams, figures, images, tables, and other information used in this publication are either created by us, obtained with permission, or fall under fair use guidelines. However, if any copyright infringement has inadvertently occurred, please notify us promptly at thinknetic@mail.net, providing sufficient details to identify the specific material in question. We will take immediate action to rectify the situation, which may include obtaining necessary permissions, making corrections, or removing the material in subsequent editions or reprints.